T0291342

AMERICAN POLITICAL, ECONOMIC, AND SECURITY ISSUES

IDENTITY THEFT TAX REFUND FRAUD

CHALLENGES AND REDUCTION EFFORTS

AMERICAN POLITICAL, ECONOMIC, AND SECURITY ISSUES

Additional books in this series can be found on Nova's website
under the Series tab.

Additional e-books in this series can be found on Nova's website
under the e-book tab.

IDENTITY THEFT TAX REFUND FRAUD

CHALLENGES AND REDUCTION EFFORTS

LUCAS HAYNES
EDITOR

publishers

New York

Copyright © 2015 by Nova Science Publishers, Inc.

NOTICE TO THE READER

Library of Congress Cataloging-in-Publication Data

ISBN: 978-1-63482-602-0

Published by Nova Science Publishers, Inc. † New York

CONTENTS

Preface   **vii**

Chapter 1   Identity Theft: Additional Actions Could
                  Help IRS Combat the Large, Evolving
                  Threat of Refund Fraud   **1**
                  United States Government Accountability Office

Chapter 2   Identity Theft and Tax Fraud:
                  Enhanced Authentication Could Combat
                  Refund Fraud, but IRS Lacks an Estimate of Costs,
                  Benefits and Risks   **39**
                  United States Government Accountability Office

Chapter 3   Prisoner Tax Refund Fraud: Delays Continue
                  in Completing Agreements to Share
                  Information with Prisons, and Reports to
                  Congress Are Not Timely or Complete   **87**
                  Treasury Inspector General for Tax Administration

Index   **121**

PREFACE

This book examines what IRS knows about the extent of IDT refund fraud and additional actions IRS can take to combat IDT refund fraud using third-party information from, for example, employers and financial institutions. The book also assesses the quality of IRS's IDT refund fraud cost estimates, and IRS's progress in developing processes to enhance taxpayer authentication.

Chapter 1 – Identity theft tax refund fraud is a persistent, evolving threat to honest taxpayers and tax administration. It occurs when an identity thief files a fraudulent tax return using a legitimate taxpayer's identifying information and claims a refund.

GAO was asked to review IRS's efforts to combat IDT refund fraud. This report, the first of a series, examines (1) what IRS knows about the extent of IDT refund fraud and (2) additional actions IRS can take to combat IDT refund fraud using third-party information from, for example, employers and financial institutions.

To understand what is known about the extent of IDT refund fraud, GAO reviewed IRS documentation, including the *Identity Theft Taxonomy*. To identify additional actions IRS can take, GAO assessed IRS and SSA data on the timing of W-2s; and interviewed SSA officials and selected associations representing software companies, return preparers, payroll companies, and others.

Chapter 2 – IRS estimated it prevented $24.2 billion in fraudulent identity theft (IDT) refunds in 2013, but paid $5.8 billion later determined to be fraud. Because of the difficulties in knowing the amount of undetected fraud, the actual amount could differ from these point estimates. IDT refund fraud occurs when an identity thief uses a legitimate taxpayer's identifying information to file a fraudulent tax return and claims a refund.

GAO was asked to review IRS's efforts to combat IDT refund fraud. This report, the second in a series, assesses (1) the quality of IRS's IDT refund fraud cost estimates, and (2) IRS's progress in developing processes to enhance taxpayer authentication.

GAO compared IRS's IDT estimate methodology to *GAO Cost Guide* best practices (fraud is a cost to taxpayers). To assess IRS's progress enhancing authentication, GAO reviewed IRS documentation and interviewed IRS officials, other government officials, and associations representing software companies, return preparers, and financial institutions.

Chapter 3 – Refund fraud associated with prisoner Social Security numbers remains a significant problem for tax administration. The number of fraudulent tax returns filed using a prisoner's Social Security number that were identified by the IRS increased from more than 37,000 tax returns in Calendar Year 2007 to more than 137,000 tax returns in Calendar Year 2012. The refunds claimed on these tax returns increased from $166 million to $1 billion. The objective of this report was to evaluate the effectiveness of the IRS's corrective actions to identify and reduce prisoner fraud.

In: Identity Theft Tax Refund Fraud   ISBN: 978-1-63482-602-0
Editor: Lucas Haynes   © 2015 Nova Science Publishers, Inc.

Chapter 1

IDENTITY THEFT: ADDITIONAL ACTIONS COULD HELP IRS COMBAT THE LARGE, EVOLVING THREAT OF REFUND FRAUD[*]

United States Government Accountability Office

ABBREVIATIONS

CDW	Compliance Data Warehouse
DDb	Dependent Database
EFDS	Electronic Fraud Detection System
e-file	electronically file
IDT	identity theft
IP PIN	Identity Protection Personal Identification Number
IRS	Internal Revenue Service
RRP	Return Review Program
SSA	Social Security Administration
SSN	Social Security number
Taxonomy	IRS *Identity Theft Taxonomy*
Treasury	Department of the Treasury
W-2	Form W-2, *Wage and Tax Statement*
W-2c	Form W-2c, *Corrected Wage and Tax Statement*

---

[*] This is an edited, reformatted and augmented version of The United States Government Accountability Office publication, GAO-14-633, dated August 2014.

WHY GAO DID THIS STUDY

Identity theft tax refund fraud is a persistent, evolving threat to honest taxpayers and tax administration. It occurs when an identity thief files a fraudulent tax return using a legitimate taxpayer's identifying information and claims a refund.

GAO was asked to review IRS's efforts to combat IDT refund fraud. This report, the first of a series, examines (1) what IRS knows about the extent of IDT refund fraud and (2) additional actions IRS can take to combat IDT refund fraud using third-party information from, for example, employers and financial institutions.

To understand what is known about the extent of IDT refund fraud, GAO reviewed IRS documentation, including the *Identity Theft Taxonomy*. To identify additional actions IRS can take, GAO assessed IRS and SSA data on the timing of W-2s; and interviewed SSA officials and selected associations representing software companies, return preparers, payroll companies, and others.

WHAT GAO RECOMMENDS

GAO recommends that Congress should consider providing Treasury with authority to lower the annual threshold for e-filing W-2s. In addition, IRS should fully assess the costs and benefits of shifting W-2 deadlines, and provide this information to Congress. IRS neither agreed nor disagreed with GAO's recommendations, and it stated it is determining how these potential corrective actions align with available resources and IRS priorities.

WHAT GAO FOUND

Based on preliminary analysis, the Internal Revenue Service (IRS) estimates it paid $5.2 billion in fraudulent identity theft (IDT) refunds in filing season 2013, while preventing $24.2 billion (based on what it could detect). The full extent is unknown because of the challenges inherent in detecting IDT refund fraud.

IDT refund fraud takes advantage of IRS's "look-back" compliance model. Under this model, rather than holding refunds until completing all compliance checks, IRS issues refunds after conducting selected reviews. While there are no simple solutions, one option is earlier matching of employer-reported wage information to taxpayers' returns before issuing refunds. IRS currently cannot do such matching because employers' wage data (from Form W-2s) are not available until months after IRS issues most refunds. Consequently, IRS begins matching employer-reported W-2 data to tax returns in July, following the tax season. If IRS had access to W-2 data earlier—through accelerated W-2 deadlines and increased electronic filing of W-2s—it could conduct pre-refund matching and identify discrepancies to prevent the issuance of billions in fraudulent refunds.

Time Delay Between Refund Issuance and IRS W-2 Posting Date, Filing Season 2012

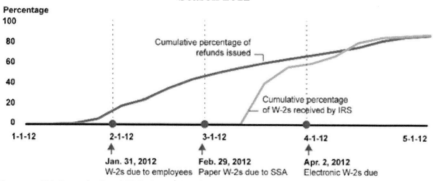

Source: GAO analysis of IRS data. | GAO-14-633.

Accelerated W-2 deadlines. In 2014, the Department of the Treasury (Treasury) proposed that Congress accelerate W-2 deadlines to January 31. However, IRS has not fully assessed the impacts of this proposal. Without this assessment, Congress does not have the information needed to deliberate the merits of such a significant change to W-2 deadlines or the use of pre-refund W-2 matching. Such an assessment is consistent with IRS's strategic plan that calls for analytics-based decisions, and would help IRS ensure effective use of resources.

Increased e-filing of W-2s. Treasury has requested authority to reduce the 250- return threshold for electronically filing (e-filing) information returns. The Social Security Administration (SSA) estimated that to meaningfully increase W-2 e-filing, the threshold would have to be lowered to include those filing 5 to 10 W-2s. In addition, SSA estimated an administrative cost savings of about $0.50 per e-filed W-2. Based on these cost savings and the ancillary benefits they provide in supporting IRS's efforts to conduct more pre-refund matching, a change in the e-filing threshold is warranted. Without this change, some employers' paper W-2s could not be available for IRS matching until much later in the year, due to the additional time needed to process paper forms.

* * *

August 20, 2014

The Honorable Ron Wyden
Chairman

The Honorable Orrin Hatch
Ranking Member
Committee on Finance
United States Senate

The Honorable Bill Nelson
Chairman

The Honorable Susan M. Collins
Ranking Member
Special Committee on Aging
United States Senate

The Honorable Dave Camp
Chairman
Committee on Ways and Means
House of Representatives

Tax refund fraud associated with identity theft (IDT) continues to be an evolving threat, one that imposes a serious financial and emotional toll on honest taxpayers and threatens the integrity of the tax administration system. Within the tax system, IDT refund fraud occurs when a refund-seeking identity thief files a fraudulent tax return using a legitimate taxpayer's identifying information. The Internal Revenue Service (IRS) estimates that millions of IDT refund fraud attempts claiming tens of billions of dollars in fraudulent refunds occurred in 2013. IDT refund fraud also creates administrative costs:

In 2014, IRS has approximately 3,000 people working on cases of IDT victims—more than twice the number of people working on these cases in 2011. In light of this, IRS recognized refund fraud and IDT as a major challenge affecting the agency in its recently issued strategic plan.[1]

To craft a response to IDT refund fraud, IRS must understand the extent and nature of the fraud. In 2012, we reported that IRS managers did not have a complete picture.[2] For example, IRS did not know the full extent of IDT refund fraud, nor did IRS systematically track the characteristics of known identity theft tax returns. While complete knowledge about identities stolen and perpetrators responsible will likely never be attained, the more thoroughly IRS understands the problem, the more effectively IRS and policymakers can respond.

IRS has taken a number of steps to address this threat, including developing an estimate of the extent of IDT refund fraud and using third-party information (such as leads about suspicious refunds) to help in its IDT efforts. However, available information suggests that the problem is persistent and evolving.

Within this context, you asked us to examine IRS's efforts to combat IDT refund fraud, which we will review in a series of reports. This report answers the following questions:

1. What does IRS know about the extent of IDT refund fraud?
2. What additional actions can IRS take to combat IDT refund fraud using third-party information (for example, from employers and financial institutions)?

A report to be issued later in 2014 will address a broader set of actions that IRS could take to combat IDT refund fraud.

To understand what IRS knows about the extent of IDT refund fraud, we reviewed IRS's *Identity Theft Taxonomy (Taxonomy)*—a matrix of IDT refund fraud categories—which estimates the amount of IDT refund fraud that IRS is, and is not, preventing. We conducted manual data testing for obvious errors and compared underlying data to IRS's *Refund Fraud & Identity Theft Global Report*. We confirmed *Taxonomy* components where we had data available to cross check. We also interviewed IRS officials to better understand the methodology used to create the estimates. For a summary of *Taxonomy* limitations, see appendix I.

To identify opportunities to improve IRS's IDT refund fraud efforts, we reviewed Internal Revenue Manual sections detailing IRS's Identity Protection

Program and IRS documentation for its External Leads Program (where third parties, often financial institutions, report suspicious refunds to IRS), Opt-In Program (where financial institutions can flag and reject suspicious refunds sent via direct deposit), and other third-party efforts. We interviewed officials from the Social Security Administration (SSA) and from associations representing software companies, return preparers, financial institutions, and payroll companies. To help ensure our analysis covered a variety of viewpoints, we selected a nonprobability sample of 22 associations and stakeholders with differing positions and characteristics, based on IRS documentation and suggestions, prior GAO work, and other information. Because we used a nonprobability sample, the views of these associations are not generalizable to all potential third parties. We then communicated with IRS offices, including (1) Privacy, Government Liaison, and Disclosure; and (2) Return Integrity and Correspondence Services, to determine the feasibility of various options and the challenges of pursuing them. See appendix II for details on our scope and methodology.

We conducted this performance audit from May 2014 to August 2014 in accordance with generally accepted government auditing standards. Those standards require that we plan and perform the audit to obtain sufficient, appropriate evidence to provide a reasonable basis for our findings and conclusions based on our audit objectives. We believe that the evidence obtained provides a reasonable basis for our findings and conclusions based on our audit objectives.

BACKGROUND

IRS has reported a substantial increase in IDT refund fraud; however, it is unclear whether this reported increase is due to an overall increase in IDT refund fraud, to an improvement in IRS's ability to detect IDT refund fraud, or to a combination of the two. For example, IRS instituted IDT filters in 2012, which helped IRS find additional IDT incidents, but it is not known how much of the reported increase can be attributed to filters or to an increase in IDT refund fraud.

There are two types of tax-related IDT fraud: (1) refund fraud and (2) employment fraud. IDT refund fraud occurs when a refund-seeking identity thief files a fraudulent tax return using the legitimate taxpayer's identifying information. Employment fraud occurs when an identity thief uses a taxpayer's name and Social Security number (SSN) to obtain a job. This report's discussion focuses on IDT refund fraud and not employment fraud.

IDT refund fraud takes advantage of the typical process of filing a tax return. Taxpayers receive information returns from third parties, such as the Form W-2, *Wage and Tax Statement* (W-2), and use this information to complete their tax returns. As shown in figure 1, taxpayers with wage income typically receive a Form W-2 from their employer by late January. Taxpayers copy the information from the W-2 to prepare their returns. Taxpayers filing paper returns are required to attach a copy of the W-2 to the return. Taxpayers filing electronically (e-file), as most do, are not required to send W-2s to the IRS. Most taxpayers entitled to a refund, along with many identity thieves attempting refund fraud, file early in the filing season—many in February. During return processing, IRS performs some compliance checks and issues refunds, but at this time it cannot verify the W-2 information for all returns (paper W-2s can be forged and fictitious wage information can be entered on a tax return).[3] By the end of March, employers are also required to send a copy of the W-2 to SSA, which performs verification checks before sending the information to IRS.[4] However, IRS only begins matching W-2 information from employers to tax returns in July. This gap between when IRS issues refunds and when IRS matches W-2s to tax returns creates the opportunity for fraudsters to file returns using a stolen identity and to receive a tax refund.

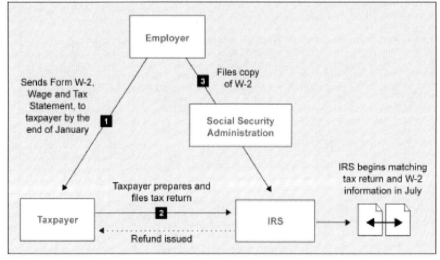

Source: GAO analysis of IRS documents. | GAO-14-633.

Figure 1. Example of the Typical Process for Filing a Tax Return.

Issuing refunds before fully verifying the information on tax returns is an example of what IRS officials refer to as a "look-back" compliance model: rather than holding refunds until all compliance checks can be completed, IRS issues refunds after doing some selected, automated reviews of the information the taxpayer submits to verify identity (e.g., name and SSN matching); filtering out returns with indicators of fraud such as a mismatched name and SSN; and correcting obvious errors, such as calculation mistakes and claims for credits and deductions exceeding statutory limits. IRS's intent is to issue refunds quickly.[5]

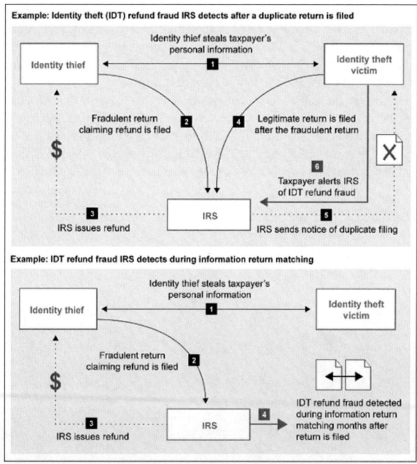

Source: GAO analysis of IRS documents. | GAO-14-633.
Note: Numbers represent the order in which these actions occur in the examples.

Figure 2. Examples of Identity Theft Refund Fraud That IRS Detects.

After refunds are issued, IRS does further checks. Two of these checks enable IRS to detect significant amounts of IDT refund fraud after the fact. One, shown at the top of figure 2, is checking for duplicate returns. If an identity thief and a legitimate taxpayer file returns using the same name and SSN, IRS will have duplicate returns. The other is matching tax returns to third-party information provided to IRS by employers, financial institutions, and others (bottom of figure 2). Matching tax returns to W-2s is an example of these checks. As we have reported, these post-refund compliance checks can take a year or more to complete.[6]

IRS Tools to Combat Identity Theft Refund Fraud

Recognizing the limitations of the look-back compliance model, IRS's efforts to combat IDT refund fraud occur at three different stages of the refund process: (1) before accepting a tax return, (2) during tax return processing, and (3) after issuing tax refunds. At each stage of the process, IRS uses specific tools to detect IDT refund fraud (see figure 3 for examples of IRS tools at each stage).

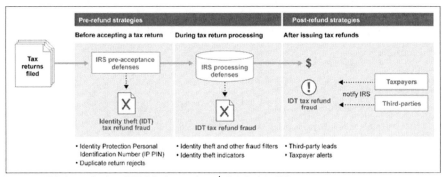

Source: GAO analysis of IRS information. | GAO-14-633.

Figure 3. Examples of IRS Tools Used to Combat Identity Theft Refund Fraud, by Processing Stage.

Before Accepting a Tax Return (Pre-Acceptance)

Identity Protection Personal Identification Number (IP PIN)

IP PINs are single-use identification numbers sent to IDT victims who have validated their identities with IRS. Tax returns with IP PINs pass through

IRS's IDT fraud filters, avoiding false positives—where a legitimate taxpayer is identified as an identity thief—and a delayed tax refund. Taxpayers who were issued an IP PIN but e-filed without using it or entered it incorrectly are prompted to enter the IP PIN on their tax return or to file on paper, according to IRS officials. Paper returns filed with the SSN of these taxpayers and without an IP PIN are subject to additional checks. (In January 2014, IRS offered a limited IP PIN pilot program to eligible taxpayers in Florida, Georgia, and the District of Columbia.)

Duplicate Return Rejects

Once IRS receives an e-filed return for a given SSN, it automatically rejects subsequent returns filed using that SSN and sends a notice of duplicate filing, as shown at the top of figure 2.[7]

During Tax Return Processing

IDT and Other Fraud Filters

IDT filters screen returns, using characteristics that IRS has identified in previous IDT refund fraud schemes.[8] The filters also search for clusters of returns with similar characteristics, such as the same bank account or address, which could indicate potential fraud. If an IDT filter flags a return, IRS stops processing the return and sends a letter asking the taxpayer to validate his or her identity.

IDT Indicators

Indicators—account flags that are visible to all IRS personnel with account access—are a key tool IRS uses to resolve and detect IDT. IRS uses different indicators (e.g., to denote whether the incident was identified by the IRS or a taxpayer), depending on the circumstances in which IRS learns of an identity theft-related problem.

After Issuing Refunds (Post-Refund)

Third-Party Leads

IRS receives third-party leads regarding suspected IDT refund fraud and other types of refund fraud through efforts including the External Leads Program and the Opt-In Program. The External Leads Program involves third parties providing lead information to IRS. If a questionable refund is confirmed as fraudulent, IRS requests that the financial institution return the refund. The Opt-In Program allows financial institutions to electronically reject suspicious refunds and return them to IRS, indicating why the institution is rejecting the refunds.

Taxpayer Alerts

IRS often identifies IDT refund fraud after receiving a phone call from a taxpayer who cannot file because an identity thief already filed with the SSN (i.e., a duplicate return) or because the taxpayer received a notice from IRS. For example, IRS can discover IDT when a taxpayer responds to an IRS compliance notice stating that the IRS has income and/or payment information that does not match the information reported by the taxpayer on his return.

Performance Management Information and Controls Help Agencies Assure Results and Best Use of Federal Resources

A key practice in results-oriented management of federal agencies is the establishment of agency-wide, long-term strategic goals. IRS's strategic plan for fiscal years 2014-2017 identifies two strategic goals: (1) deliver high quality and timely service to reduce taxpayer burden and encourage voluntary compliance and (2) effectively enforce the law to ensure compliance with tax responsibilities and combat fraud. The strategic plan also outlines several objectives relevant to its efforts to combat identity theft, including

- strengthening refund fraud prevention by balancing the speed of refund delivery with the assurance of taxpayer identity, using analysis of third-party and historical taxpayer data, and educating taxpayers and tax professionals on fraud risk factors and fraud prevention methods;
- implementing enterprise-wide analytics and research capabilities to make timely, informed decisions; and
- implementing and maintaining a robust enterprise risk management program, which includes establishing routine reporting procedures to external stakeholders on operational risks.

As a complement to the potential benefits of strategic planning, internal control is a major part of managing an organization.[9] Internal control comprises the plans, methods, and procedures used to meet missions, goals, and objectives: this supports performance-based management. Internal control helps agency program managers achieve desired results and provides reasonable assurance that program objectives are being achieved through— among other things—effective and efficient use of agency resources. Managers are to design internal controls based on related costs and benefits. In addition, internal control standards in the federal government call for agencies to record and communicate relevant, reliable, and timely information on internal and external events to agency managers and others who need it.

IN FILING SEASON 2013, IRS ESTIMATES PAYING $5.2 BILLION IN FRAUDULENT IDT REFUNDS WHILE PREVENTING $24.2 BILLION; HOWEVER, THE FULL EXTENT OF IDT REFUND FRAUD IS UNKNOWN

Based on IRS's preliminary *Identity Theft Taxonomy (Taxonomy),* the agency estimated that $29.4 billion in IDT refund fraud was attempted in filing season 2013. IRS estimated it prevented or recovered about $24.2 billion (82 percent) of the estimated attempted refund fraud. However, IRS estimated it paid $5.2 billion (18 percent) in IDT refunds during the same timeframe (see figure 4). IRS officials noted that they are updating their analysis and anticipate revising the *Taxonomy's* estimate of IDT refunds paid. The officials said the revised estimates could be somewhat higher (perhaps by $0.6 billion) but the analysis was not completed in time for us to include it in figure 4.

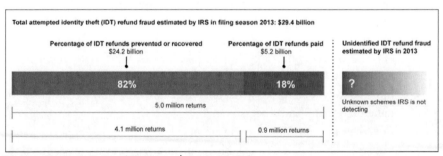

Source: GAO analysis of IRS data. | GAO-14-633.

Figure 4. IRS Preliminary Estimates of Attempted Identity Theft Refund Fraud, Filing Season 2013.

IRS's *Taxonomy* demonstrates a significant effort on the part of IRS and is an important first step in estimating how much *identified* IDT refund fraud IRS is stopping or failing to stop. IRS has made substantial progress in its efforts to estimate IDT refund fraud. For example, IRS developed an estimate of IDT refund fraud by identifying characteristics of fraudulent returns, matching and analyzing information returns and tax returns based on these characteristics, and researching other sources.

However, the estimates will continue to evolve as IRS updates its methodology to better reflect new IDT refund fraud schemes and to improve the accuracy of its estimates, according to IRS officials.[10]

IRS's *Taxonomy* is a valuable tool to help inventory, characterize, and analyze available IDT refund fraud data and to assess the performance of IRS's IDT refund fraud defenses. For example, the *Taxonomy* may help IRS

- *Monitor progress.* Given the evolving, persistent nature of IDT refund fraud, IRS will constantly need to monitor and adapt its IDT defenses to protect against new and emerging schemes. The *Taxonomy* provides IRS with a methodology for monitoring IDT refund fraud and the progress of IRS defenses over time. However, IRS will continue to face challenges in evaluating its defenses. For example, it is difficult to differentiate whether an increase in returns detected by the IDT filters is due to improved filter performance or to an increase in the overall number of IDT refund fraud attempts. In addition, future methodology updates which reflect evolving schemes and improve accuracy could make comparisons between filing seasons difficult.

- *Identify schemes.* The *Taxonomy* may help IRS develop a better understanding of taxpayer characteristics related to current, successful IDT refund fraud, including filing status, the size of the refund, filing method, and filing history. This could help IRS identify IDT refund fraud scheme trends and assist it in further developing and modifying its defenses.

- *Communicate the extent of the problem to stakeholders.* While the *Taxonomy* has limitations, it may help improve IRS managers' understanding of the problem, allowing them to better communicate with policymakers about schemes and resource needs. It may also improve the ability of Congress (and other decision makers) to oversee IRS's efforts. In addition, the data collected could be of use to IRS partners, including tax preparers and financial institutions.

Although IRS's *Taxonomy* estimates are valuable in helping estimate IDT refund fraud, they are, by their nature, incomplete. This is in part because

IRS's estimate of IDT refunds paid (the $5.2 billion shown in figure 4) is based on duplicate returns, information return mismatches, and criminal investigations identified after the refunds are paid. However, for cases where there are no duplicate returns, information returns, or criminal investigations associated with a tax return, IRS has been unable to estimate the amount of IDT refund fraud (the *unidentified* IDT refund fraud shown in figure 4). Also, certain *Taxonomy* estimates are based on assumptions using the characteristics of past IDT refund fraud. While the assumptions are based on IRS's research from known cases and appear reasonable, we could not verify the accuracy and comprehensiveness of these assumptions. This is because the accuracy of the *Taxonomy* estimates is largely based on whether the estimate includes all true IDT refund fraud returns and excludes all legitimate returns. IRS officials acknowledged their estimates for returns flagged during information return matching could include legitimate returns that are not actual IDT refund fraud.

Other limitations[11] that we identified in the *Taxonomy* include the following:

- *The Taxonomy underestimates the number of IDT refund fraud returns and refund amounts for some IDT categories and overestimates others.* The Taxonomy underestimates IDT refund fraud because, as previously discussed, IRS has been unable to estimate the amount of IDT refund fraud for cases where there are no criminal investigations, duplicate returns, or information returns— such as a W-2—associated with a tax return (the unidentified IDT refund fraud shown in figure 4). An example of an overestimated category is that of "refunds recovered," which includes refunds returned to IRS as a result of external leads. However, IRS data on external leads do not distinguish whether the type of fraud was IDT refund fraud or some other type of fraud. Our analysis of the Taxonomy found that IRS did not adjust its estimate to account for other types of refund fraud.

- *While IRS provided Taxonomy estimates for filing seasons 2012 and 2013, methodology changes make it difficult to compare these estimates over time.* For example, the filing season 2013 estimate uses a different data source to estimate the number of IDT refunds paid and eventually detected after the filing season (when IRS matches tax returns to information return data, such as W-2s). In addition, it is unclear whether changes in the number of IDT refund fraud returns are due to overall changes in fraud patterns, such as an increase or decrease in fraud attempts; to improvements in IRS IDT defenses; or to identity thieves' ability to file returns using schemes IRS has not yet learned to detect.

STRONGER PRE-REFUND AND POST-REFUND STRATEGIES CAN HELP COMBAT IDT REFUND FRAUD

IRS has responded to the problem of IDT refund fraud with new ways to combat fraud. However, according to IRS officials, identity thieves are "adaptive adversaries" who are constantly learning and changing their tactics as IRS develops new IDT strategies. Therefore, IDT refund fraud remains a persistent, evolving threat that requires stronger pre-refund and post-refund strategies to combat.

A robust pre-refund strategy is important because preventing fraudulent refunds is easier and more cost-effective than trying to recover them after they have been issued. We have previously reported that implementing strong preventive controls can help defend against invalid payments, increasing public confidence and avoiding the difficult "pay and chase" aspects of recovering invalid refunds.[12] According to IRS, the agency's Return Review Program (RRP) is one way that IRS is trying to improve its pre-refund detection efforts.[13] As IRS processes tax returns, other strategies can assist in identifying and stopping suspicious refunds. Moreover, improving post-refund programs may help IRS work with financial institutions to stop refunds that earlier controls have missed. However, recapturing a fraudulent refund after it is issued can be challenging—if not impossible—because identity thieves often spend or transfer the funds immediately, making them very difficult to trace.

Agency officials and third-party stakeholders we spoke to identified the following potential pre- and post-refund strategies that may help IRS combat IDT refund fraud:

- *Pre-refund.* Improve W-2 matching by (1) adjusting W-2 deadlines, (2) lowering the threshold for e-filed W-2s,[14] (3) delaying refunds, and (4) delaying the filing season.
- *Post-refund.* Improve external leads programs by providing timely, accurate, and actionable feedback to third parties.

Earlier, Pre-Refund W-2 Matching May Prevent Billions of Dollars in Estimated IDT Refund Fraud but Would Involve Costs

Characteristics of the current tax processing system hamper IRS's ability to effectively verify taxpayer information prior to issuing refunds. As part of a broader proposal, the Department of the Treasury (Treasury) has proposed accelerating W-2 deadlines. This proposal will help ensure that IRS has accurate, timely W-2 data to conduct pre-refund matching. IRS has also requested funding to support timelier processing of W-2s.

IRS issues most refunds before it has access to employers' W-2 data. IRS issues most refunds months before receiving and matching information returns, such as W-2s. For 2012, IRS received more than 148.3 million tax returns and issued more than $309.6 billion in refunds to 110.5 million taxpayers. By March 1, 2012 IRS had issued about 50 percent of all 2012 refunds, but did not have access to most of the 2012 W-2 data verified by the Social Security Administration (SSA) (see figure 5).[15] As previously noted, IRS's look-back compliance model does not allow it to match tax returns to information returns until early summer.

IRS is under pressure to issue refunds promptly. IRS is required by law to pay interest if it takes longer than 45 days after the due date of the return to issue a refund.[16] IRS informs taxpayers to anticipate their refunds generally within 21 days after filing and actively tries to meet this target. For tax year 2013, IRS reported that for tax returns filed through early March, taxpayers received refunds an average of 9.6 days after filing.[17]

Treasury's Proposal for Accelerated W-2 Deadlines is Intended to Benefit IRS and Taxpayers

To facilitate the use of W-2 information in detection of noncompliance (which includes IDT refund fraud) earlier in the filing season, Treasury recently proposed to Congress that the W-2 deadlines be moved to January 31 (for both paper and e-filing).[18] IRS also requested funding for processing W-2s more quickly as part of its fiscal year 2015 budget request.[19] The IRS Commissioner has also advocated for earlier deadlines, testifying that challenges with IDT refund fraud have led IRS to propose an accelerated W-2 filing deadline.[20]

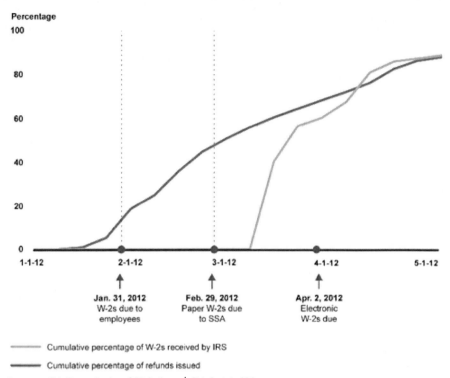

Source: GAO analysis of IRS data. | GAO-14-633.

Figure 5. Time Delay Between Refund Issuance and IRS W-2 Posting Date, Filing Season 2012.

Further, the National Taxpayer Advocate has repeatedly written about the need to develop an accelerated information reporting system to enable IRS to match third-party reports to return data before issuing refunds.[21]

According to IRS officials, earlier, pre-refund W-2 matching would provide a number of benefits, including

- *Combating IDT refund fraud.* According to IRS officials, having earlier access to W-2s, and time to match W-2s to tax returns before issuing refunds, would give IRS more opportunities to prevent billions of dollars of IDT refund fraud.[22] Returns flagged during IRS's information return matching make up a substantial portion of the $5.2 billion in IDT refunds that IRS estimated it paid in filing season 2013, according to IRS's *Taxonomy*. With earlier access to W-2 data, IRS could validate information reported on a tax return (e.g., wages and compensation) with information reported by employers before issuing refunds.[23] Even without automatic matching, IRS officials said that earlier W-2 data would speed up manual reviews of high-risk returns—such such as those flagged by the IDT filters—because the information they rely on to perform those checks would be readily available.

- *Benefiting taxpayers and employers.* In addition to protecting revenue, accelerated W-2 reporting and pre-refund matching could improve taxpayer service and reduce burden. IRS officials said that having W-2 data at the beginning of the filing season would reduce taxpayer burden by allowing IRS to verify income immediately and to release legitimate tax returns caught by the IDT filters (false positives). Earlier W-2 data could also help IRS reduce employer burden, as IRS would no longer have to contact employers of taxpayers whose returns are flagged by IDT and other fraud filters.
- *Providing other benefits.* Earlier W-2 matching could reduce IRS's workload of collection cases and help taxpayers avoid penalties and interest on under-paid taxes, according to IRS officials.

Accelerated W-2 Deadlines Could Create Other Challenges that Would Need to be Addressed

Implementing accelerated W-2 deadlines could result in an increased number of corrected W-2s filed as well as other technical and logistical challenges. SSA officials and all three payroll and information reporting associations we interviewed told us that accelerating the W-2 deadline would increase the number of corrected W-2s.[24] (These are W-2s that employers correct after sending the first incorrect version to SSA.) Corrected W-2s represent less than 1 percent of the 213.5 million W-2s IRS received from SSA in tax year 2011, according to IRS data. The correction rate is currently low because the deadlines for filing with SSA are well after the January 31 deadline for sending W-2s to employees, giving employers a window of time to make corrections before they file with SSA. Based on data tracking payroll submissions and subsequent adjustments, the National Payroll Reporting Consortium estimated that should the deadline be accelerated to before January 31, corrections may increase from 1 percent of filed W-2s to greater than 6 percent.[25] To mitigate potential corrections, SSA officials and all three payroll and information reporting associations we interviewed recommended allowing a corrections window of time (e.g., 1 to 2 weeks) between submission to employees and to SSA.

While most W-2s are filed in a timely manner, SSA currently receives some W-2s after the March 31 deadline for submitting e-filed returns. 26 For tax year 2012, SSA received 16 percent (36.5 million of 233.2 million) of W-2s after April 5, 2013.[27] According to SSA officials, employers may submit W-2s to SSA after the filing deadline for several reasons, including (for example) human error, resubmittal of an e-filed submission previously rejected by SSA, or to report back pay under a court order. In addition, according to SSA officials, moving deadlines to January 31 or earlier would create logistical and technical challenges for SSA; however, moving the e-file deadline up to the end of February would not create issues. For example, SSA officials told us that moving the deadline to January 31 or earlier would require shifting its software development cycle because SSA's computer experts are working on another system during that timeframe; however, the computer experts are available to implement an accelerated W-2 filing date of February 29.

The Costs and Benefits of Accelerated W-2 Deadlines and Pre-Refund Matching Have Not Been Assessed Fully

While Treasury and IRS officials have proposed moving up W-2 deadlines, the costs and benefits have not been identified, estimated, or documented. How IRS decides to implement pre-refund matching using W-2 data would affect the costs and benefits for itself and other stakeholders. Some of the stakeholder issues that we identified and that remain unaddressed include the following:

- *IRS.* IRS has not identified cost-effective options for updating the information technology systems or work processes (such as the process for correcting refund amounts if mismatches are detected) needed to implement pre-refund matching using W-2 data. IRS officials said that a lack of budgetary resources is the primary reason IRS has not conducted planning and analysis of the costs and benefits related to accelerating W-2 deadlines. The full costs will not be known until IRS analyzes details regarding how the agency would implement this change (e.g., the thresholds IRS uses to match W-2s will influence the number of W-2 mismatches due to IDT refund fraud or false positives, where legitimate returns are flagged during matching). Similarly, IRS does not have a well-developed estimate of the magnitude of the benefits of pre-refund W-2 matching. Treasury developed revenue projections for moving all information reporting deadlines, but did not develop projections specific to the W-2 deadline. While IRS has a basis for estimating the revenue protected from pre-refund matching (from its *Taxonomy*), other benefits—such as employer savings from fewer queries from IRS—may be harder to estimate.

- *SSA.* Moving the deadline to January 31 would create logistical and technical challenges for SSA. As previously discussed, SSA officials told us that moving the deadline to January 31 or earlier would require shifting its software development cycle because SSA's computer experts are working on another system during that timeframe; however, the computer experts are available to implement an accelerated W-2 filing date of February 29. If concurrent changes in the e-file threshold are not made, SSA may also incur administrative costs, should the number of W-2 corrections increase or a processing backlog occur (see next section for details).

- *Third parties.* The costs and benefits to employers and payroll providers have not been quantified. SSA officials stated that moving any W-2 deadline (other than the current e-file deadline of March 31) involves a degree of risk that cannot be quantified at present. They recommended surveying employers and payroll providers to better understand the impact of shortening or eliminating the time gap between when W-2s must be provided to employees and when they must be provided to SSA.

Estimating the costs and benefits of options to accelerate W-2 deadlines and to conduct earlier W-2 matching is consistent with IRS's strategic plan, which includes objectives to strengthen refund fraud prevention through the use of third-party data and to use analytics for timely, informed decision making.[28] It is also consistent with *Standards for Internal Control in the Federal Government*, which calls for IRS management to design and implement internal controls within its programs based on the related costs and benefits.[29] However, without better analysis of the costs and benefits of options for implementing accelerated W-2 deadlines and pre-refund matching, Congress does not have the information needed to consider Treasury's proposal and deliberate the merits of making such a significant change.

Other Policy Changes May Be Needed to Implement Earlier, Pre-Refund W-2 Matching

Agency officials and third-party stakeholders we spoke to noted that other policy changes may also be needed in concert with moving W-2 deadlines.

This is because W-2 matching is part of a much larger tax-administration system that provides IRS with information needed to help verify the identity, employment, and earnings of taxpayers. These changes could include lowering the e-file threshold for employers, delaying refunds, or delaying the start of the filing season. IRS has not yet undertaken efforts to understand the full costs of implementing earlier, pre-refund W-2 matching, and the costs associated with these other changes.

Lowering the E-File Threshold for Employers

Because of the additional time and resources associated with processing paper W-2s submitted by employers, SSA officials told us that a change in the e-file threshold would be needed to sufficiently increase the number of e-filed W-2s. Reducing the e-file threshold would allow IRS to obtain timely, accurate data from a significant number of employers and would enhance the benefits IRS could obtain from the accelerated W-2 deadline and pre-refund W-2 matching. Currently, employers who file 250 or more W-2s annually must e-file those forms.[30] Low-volume filers (filing fewer than 250 information returns annually) can file on paper, and for tax year 2011 these employers sent about 27.6 million paper W-2s (13 percent of all W-2s filed), according to IRS data. Because of the additional time SSA needs to process paper W-2s before sending them to IRS, changes in the e-file threshold would be necessary for earlier W-2 deadlines to have the intended effect. Without a change in the e-file threshold, backlogs in paper W-2s could result in IRS receiving W-2 data after the end of the filing season. For example, SSA officials said they can have a large backlog of paper W-2s and can process some paper W-2s as late as August or September. Having more e-filed W-2s would speed processing time for SSA (as compared to paper W-2 processing time) and would enable IRS to receive a larger percentage of W-2 data earlier, according to SSA officials.

More than 4.5 million establishments have fewer than 10 employees, [31] and SSA officials estimated that the e-file threshold would need to be reduced to 5 to 10 information returns for the change to result in a meaningful increase in the number of e-filed W-2s. Many states have already implemented lower e-file thresholds. According to the American Payroll Association, 19 states, the District of Columbia, and Puerto Rico have a W-2 e-file threshold that is lower than IRS's information return requirement.[32]

Two of the three payroll and information reporting associations we interviewed said lowering the e-file threshold would not create problems for most employers.[33] An organization representing small businesses was generally supportive of lowering the e-file threshold, but also noted that a minority of small businesses may oppose a threshold reduction. However, there are ways to mitigate the burden on small businesses, including implementing a gradual reduction in the threshold and/or allowing employers to file for hardship waivers.[34] Additionally, small employers can e-file W-2s at no cost through SSA's web application, Business Services Online.

In addition to contributing to the IRS's ability to verify employment information on tax returns, lowering the e-file threshold could reduce administrative costs for SSA. Based on fiscal year 2013 data, SSA officials stated that an e-filed W-2 costs about $0.002 to process, while a paper W-2 costs about $0.53 to transcribe and process. [35] Moreover, SSA officials said it is more difficult to ensure data quality with paper W-2s, as transcription errors can occur while processing paper W-2s.

Treasury recently requested that Congress expand legal authority to allow a reduction of the 250-return e-filing threshold for a broad set of information returns, including W-2s. [36] According to Treasury, benefits such as enhancing taxpayer compliance, improving IRS service to taxpayers, and modernizing tax administration make this change worthwhile. For example, expanding e-filing will help IRS focus its audit activities, as IRS will receive information in a useable form, according to Treasury. The cost savings described above, as well as compliance and other benefits, could be realized before Congress decides on whether to accelerate W-2 deadlines (as proposed by Treasury). The change would support IRS's strategic objectives to encourage compliance while minimizing costs and taxpayer burden.[37] In addition, increasing e-filing is consistent with internal controls, which require that information be recorded and communicated to management and others within the entity who need it and in a form and within a timeframe that enables them to carry out their internal control and other responsibilities.[38] For an entity to run and control its operations, it must have relevant, reliable, and timely communications relating to internal as well as external events.

Implementing a lower e-filing threshold would have the ancillary benefit (described above) of supporting pre-refund matching.

Delaying Refunds and Delaying the Start of the Filing Season

In conjunction with other strategies such as earlier filing of W-2s, delaying the filing season or delaying refunds would provide more time for IRS to receive W-2s, conduct pre-refund matching, and identify IDT refund fraud, according to IRS and third-party officials.[39] IRS could delay the start of the filing season—the date IRS begins to process tax returns—but changing

IRS's obligation to issue refunds within 45 days of the due date of the return would require a statutory amendment.[40] Both changes would have costs associated with educating taxpayers about the changes and potential costs to taxpayers who receive refunds later (discussed below). In our discussions with third parties about ways to prevent IDT refund fraud, 10 of the 22 groups we interviewed—ranging from financial institution associations to software companies to payroll associations— specifically suggested the option of delaying refunds or delaying the filing season until IRS could match W-2 data to tax returns.[41]

Delaying refunds is likely to burden taxpayers, according to IRS and third-party officials. Taxpayers who file early and who are financially dependent on a refund, such as low-income taxpayers receiving refundable credits, could be burdened. For example, according to the National Taxpayer Advocate, delayed refunds would have a detrimental effect on low-income taxpayers who use their tax refunds to pay winter utility bills.[42] According to our analysis, the changes would also result in a permanent shift in the annual cycle of refunds on which some taxpayers depend. Once the change is made, the time interval between annual refunds will be the same length as it is now; however, during the first year of implementation, that interval may be increased by several months. This additional waiting time in the first year could be burdensome for some taxpayers; however, there should be no added burden in subsequent years (i.e. the interval between refunds will be approximately 12 months in those later years).[43]

Weaknesses in Third-Party Partnership Programs Limit Post-Refund Fraud Detection

Through its external leads programs, IRS collaborates with financial institutions, software companies, prepaid card companies, and other third parties. These partnerships provide valuable information about emerging IDT trends and fraudulent returns that have passed through IRS's prevention and detection systems. External leads help IRS identify fraudulent refunds and understand emerging trends in IDT refund fraud and other refund fraud. According to IRS officials, the agency has used third-party leads to improve detection of IDT refund fraud.[44] Between January 1, 2014 and May 31, 2014, IRS reported that more than 350 sources sent IRS successful leads for nearly 94,000 taxpayer accounts: these leads were for all types of refund fraud including, but not limited to, IDT refund fraud.[45] IRS reported that financial institutions returned $214.8 million in fraudulent refunds during this period.

Communicating with third parties is consistent with IRS's strategic plan objective to implement a robust enterprise risk management program by establishing routine reporting procedures to inform external stakeholders about operational risks. [46] Also, it is consistent with internal controls, which require relevant, reliable, and timely communications relating to external events.[47] As such, management should ensure there are adequate means of communicating with external stakeholders and of obtaining information from them that could help IRS achieve its goal of reducing IDT refund fraud.

Disclosure constraints limit what IRS can share. Section 6103 of the Internal Revenue Code limits the types of information IRS can share with external parties, even for fraudulent returns.[48] However, section 6103 does not limit IRS's ability to share general information about how to manage IDT refund fraud or emerging fraud trends. Disclosure of individual taxpayer information could be prevented by aggregating information so that no individual taxpayers could be identified. IRS officials told us that aggregated feedback to third parties may be possible, as long as a sufficient number of leads are discussed.

IRS feedback to third parties is limited. While IRS's feedback differs by external leads program, third parties receive limited feedback across both programs.[49] Eight of the eleven financial institution and tax software associations/companies we interviewed said that IRS provides little to no feedback in response to leads sent through the External Leads Program or the Opt-In Program, or they told us they requested additional feedback from IRS. Furthermore, IRS officials told us that the agency has received millions of leads from software companies, but while IRS makes an effort to examine and address the highest priority leads (e.g., high refund dollars), IRS has not analyzed or provided feedback about many of these leads because it does not have the resources to do so. Without accurate, timely, and actionable feedback, external parties do not know if the leads they provide to IRS are useful. Five of these eleven financial institution associations and tax software associations/companies volunteered that they are not able to assess their success in identifying IDT refund fraud, or to improve their own detection tools.[50] Useful feedback may include aggregated information about the share of each institution's leads that helped to identify suspicious returns and other information about IDT refund fraud trends. This type of aggregated information would also comply with section 6103 disclosure requirements.

IRS's general and aggregated feedback is limited to particular groups.
IRS shares general information about high-level schemes and IDT refund
fraud trends during meetings with BITS, the technology policy division of the
Financial Services Roundtable.[51] However, financial institutions that are not
part of that organization may not have the opportunity to learn from these
discussions.[52] In addition, IRS officials said they provide aggregated data
about leads received to tax software companies that request the information,
but companies that do not request the information may not receive this
feedback.

IRS does not use metrics for tracking external leads. To provide aggregated
feedback by institution, IRS would need to begin tracking this information. IRS
officials said they have not implemented metrics by institution because of a
lack of resources. While IRS compiles information—including the total number
of external lead sources, leads submitted, and associated refund dollars—the
agency does not use the information to develop metrics to track leads by the
submitting third party. For the External Leads Program, IRS officials told us
that while IRS monitors the volume of leads and associated refund dollars to
assess accomplishments and program value, it does not use metrics to monitor
and follow up on leads, including the tracking of leads by the third party that
submitted them. In addition, IRS officials said while IRS provides some
overall data for the Opt-In Program, it does not track this information by
financial institution. Because IRS does not track external leads by institution,
it cannot use this information to improve IDT refund fraud programs or to
provide feedback to third parties about the effectiveness of their leads.

Strengthening IRS's partnerships with third parties would require IRS to
expend resources analyzing leads and providing feedback to third parties. These
costs could vary, depending on the systems involved and the level of feedback
IRS provides. IRS has some of the information needed to track leads in this
way. For example, spreadsheets submitted through the External Leads Program
contain the institutions' names, so entirely new data collection systems may not
be needed. Our past work has shown that developing metrics to track external
leads by submitting party is consistent with practices that enhance the use of
performance information, such as communicating that information frequently
and effectively.[53] In addition, tracking external leads would support IRS's
strategic goal of supporting effective tax administration by providing timely
information to external partners in the tax community.[54] Metrics would allow
IRS to communicate information to specific third parties, who could then adapt
their own IDT detection tools. Given the millions of dollars in refund fraud
returned by financial institutions in the first five months of 2014, even a modest

increase in IDT refunds returned due to institution-specific feedback may be worth the investment of tracking external leads.

CONCLUSION

IDT refund fraud is a large problem: IRS estimates it issued at least $5.2 billion in fraudulent IDT refunds in filing season 2013. Given the size and scope of IDT refund fraud, additional bold and innovative steps are needed from Congress and IRS. For IRS to successfully combat IDT refund fraud, it will need to develop heightened awareness in its understanding of emerging trends, and in its ability to leverage both internal and external resources. While there is no "silver bullet" available to resolve the problem, developing strategies that focus on both preventing IDT refund fraud and resolving it can help IRS respond to this evolving threat. These strategies are likely to include constantly adapting and strengthening present defenses while also developing new strategies for both electronic and paper returns that stop IDT refund fraud at all stages of return processing.

Given the billions in dollars of successful IDT refund fraud, IRS must strive to stay one or more steps ahead of identity thieves, or the risk of issuing fraudulent IDT refunds could grow. Staying ahead of identity thieves will require a significant resource investment from IRS as it strengthens and develops new tools. Accelerating the W-2 deadline to January 31—as proposed by Treasury—would provide a powerful tool for IRS to detect and prevent IDT refund fraud. At the same time, the full costs and benefits are not known because IRS has not considered how it would implement pre-refund matching using W-2 data. The burden this would impose on employers, the costs to IRS for systems changes, and the likely need for other changes (such as increased e-filing) means this step should not be taken without an informed discussion among all stakeholders, including Congress. Further, taxpayers' expectations about the filing season and when they can anticipate receiving refunds may need to shift. Also, IRS has not fully leveraged third parties, having provided only limited feedback on the IDT refund leads third parties are submitting and offering limited general information on IDT refund fraud trends. However, to provide this information, IRS will need metrics to track external leads by the third party that submitted them, which it currently does not have. While the cost of providing third-party feedback could vary depending on the level of feedback IRS provides, third-party leads returned hundreds of millions of dollars in all refund fraud to the IRS in 2014, and are a valuable information resource about fraudulent returns that have bypassed IRS's prevention and detection systems.

MATTERS FOR CONGRESSIONAL CONSIDERATION

Congress should consider providing the Secretary of the Treasury with the regulatory authority to lower the threshold for electronic filing of W-2s from 250 returns annually to between 5 to 10 returns, as appropriate.

RECOMMENDATIONS FOR EXECUTIVE ACTION

We recommend the Commissioner of Internal Revenue fully assess the costs and benefits of accelerating W-2 deadlines and provide information to Congress on

- the IRS systems and work processes that will need to be adjusted to accommodate earlier, pre-refund matching of W-2s and then identify timeframes for when these changes could be made;
- potential impacts on taxpayers, IRS, SSA, and third parties; and
- what other changes will be needed (such as delaying the start of the filing season or delaying refunds) to ensure IRS can match tax returns to W-2 data before issuing refunds.

We recommend that the Commissioner of Internal Revenue take the following two actions to provide timely, accurate, and actionable feedback to all relevant lead-generating third parties:

- provide aggregated information on (1) the success of external party leads in identifying suspicious returns and (2) emerging trends (pursuant to section 6103 restrictions); and
- develop a set of metrics to track external leads by the submitting third party.

AGENCY COMMENTS AND OUR EVALUATION

We provided a draft of this product to IRS and SSA for review and comment. In its written comments, IRS neither agreed nor disagreed with our recommendations. IRS stated that it is determining how potential corrective actions align with available resources and IRS priorities before deciding whether to implement the recommendations. With regard to our first set of recommendations, IRS acknowledged that accelerating W-2 deadlines or delaying the tax filing season represents a significant change to tax administration. IRS stated that in order to determine the best course of action, Congress needs an understanding of the costs and benefits for IRS and other stakeholders. With regard to our second set of recommendations, IRS stated that information sharing, as permitted under the law—such as providing feedback to third parties—fosters good working relationships and promotes ongoing program improvements. IRS provided technical comments that we incorporated, as appropriate.

We recognize the need for IRS to assess its priorities given the fiscal constraints it faces. We previously reported that since fiscal year 2010, IRS has absorbed approximately $900 million in budget cuts while facing increasing workloads as a result of legislative mandates and priority programs, such as work related to the Patient Protection and Affordable Care Act.[55] Even with these constraints and other potentially competing priorities, we believe the size of the IDT problem warrants additional action now. Pre-refund matching of W-2 data is one option that IRS agrees has the potential to prevent a substantial portion of the estimated $5.2 billion in IDT refunds paid in filing season 2013. However, such a change may require a significant resource investment by IRS as well as impact taxpayers and employers. Without better information about the benefits and costs of such a significant change, Congress cannot make an informed decision about implementing it. With respect to our recommendations regarding the External Leads Program, IRS highlighted the fact that the program has generated more than $2.3 billion in refunds returned to the U.S. Treasury from 2010 to 2014. Given that IRS already has some of the information needed to better track external lead results, IRS should be able to control the costs of implementing our recommendations.

In its written comments, SSA stated that its implementation of a redesigned Annual Wage Reporting system for processing W-2s in January 2015 and W-2cs in January 2016 will position the agency to support an accelerated W-2 deadline as well as support lowering the threshold for e-filing W-2s. SSA also said that it transmits wage data to IRS immediately upon receiving electronic W-2s. Paper W-2s require manual handling and therefore have a significantly longer processing time. SSA also recommended that IRS consider the impact of Form 1099 reporting in making decisions to accelerate the W-2 reporting and change IRS business processes. SSA also provided technical comments that we incorporated, as appropriate.

James R. White
Director, Tax Issues
Strategic Issues

APPENDIX I: IRS IDENTITY THEFT TAXONOMY LIMITATIONS

IRS developed the *Identity Theft Taxonomy* (*Taxonomy*) to monitor the volume of identity theft (IDT) refund fraud attempts and assess the impact of its IDT defenses over time, among other reasons. The *Taxonomy* is a matrix of IDT refund fraud categories that estimate the amount of *identified* IDT refund fraud IRS prevented or recovered, as well as the *identified* IDT refund fraud IRS paid. The estimates are based on IRS's administrative records of known IDT refund fraud (e.g., data on the number of duplicate returns or returns detected by identity theft filters). The *Taxonomy* also estimates likely identity theft by identifying returns with the characteristics of IDT refund fraud, which are found when IRS matches returns to W-2 and other information return data after the tax filing season. The *Taxonomy* is a valuable step toward inventorying available IDT refund fraud data and assessing the performance of IRS's IDT refund fraud defenses. However, we identified limitations in the *Taxonomy*, specifically

- *Taxonomy estimates are preliminary.* After we provided a draft for comment, IRS officials stated that the *Taxonomy* estimates are preliminary, as they are updating their analysis using information return matching to identify likely returns where IRS paid IDT refunds. They anticipate their estimates for IDT refunds paid will increase somewhat (perhaps by $0.6 billion), but an updated *Taxonomy* estimate was not completed in time for us to include in this report.
- *Using administrative records could result in imprecise estimates.* *Taxonomy* estimates could be imprecise because the returns identified

may not accurately represent the true universe of IDT refund fraud. If only certain kinds of criminals (or fraudsters) are more likely to be detected by IRS defenses, IRS records on detected IDT refund fraud may not accurately represent all individuals attempting to commit IDT refund fraud.

- *Certain Taxonomy estimates are based on assumptions using the characteristics of past IDT refund fraud.* While the assumptions are based on IRS's research from known cases and appear reasonable, we could not verify the accuracy and comprehensiveness of these assumptions. This is because the accuracy of the *Taxonomy* estimates is largely based on whether the estimate includes all true IDT refund fraud returns and excludes all legitimate returns. IRS officials acknowledged their estimates for returns flagged during information return matching could include legitimate returns that are not actual IDT refund fraud. For example, the estimate could include returns flagged due to taxpayer or employer error or other non-IDT fraud by taxpayers (e.g., the taxpayer deliberately enters false information on his tax return to obtain a larger refund). Changes in these assumptions can substantially affect the estimates, but this uncertainty is not reflected in IRS's *Taxonomy* estimates for filing season 2013 (e.g., IRS does not present a range of estimates based on differing assumptions).

- *IRS's Taxonomy underestimates the number of IDT refund fraud returns and refund amounts for some IDT categories.* IRS's estimate of IDT refunds paid is based on duplicate returns, information return mismatches, and criminal investigations identified after the refunds are paid. However, for cases where there are no duplicate returns, information returns, or criminal investigations associated with a tax return, IRS has been unable to estimate the amount of IDT refund fraud. IRS officials have considered using surveys to estimate unidentified IDT refund fraud, but have not been able to come up with a survey method that would avoid significant taxpayer burden.

- *IRS's Taxonomy overestimates the number of IDT refund fraud returns and refund amounts for some IDT categories.* For example, IRS's estimates for "refunds protected" include refunds returned to IRS as a result of external leads. However, IRS data on external leads do not distinguish whether the type of fraud was IDT refund fraud or some other type of fraud. Our analysis of the *Taxonomy* found that

IRS did not adjust its estimate to account for other types of refund fraud.

- *Methodology changes and other factors prevent comparisons between filing seasons 2012 and 2013 estimates.* For filing season 2012, IRS estimates it prevented or recovered about $21.6 billion (71 percent) of the estimated IDT refunds and paid $8.9 billion (29 percent). Comparing filing season 2012 and 2013 estimates is problematic because it is unclear whether the changes are due to methodological changes, such as using different data sources or changing the criteria for querying data. IRS officials said they update their methodology to better reflect evolving IDT refund fraud schemes and improve the accuracy of *Taxonomy* estimates, although they attempt to use consistent definitions to promote comparability of estimates across years. In addition, it is unclear whether changes are due to overall changes in fraud patterns, such as an increase or decrease in fraud attempts; improvements in IRS IDT defenses; or identity thieves' ability to file returns using schemes IRS has not yet learned to detect.

It is likely that IRS's estimates of the IDT refund fraud for filing seasons 2012 and 2013 will continue to evolve as IRS improves the *Taxonomy* methodology. For example, during the course of our audit, we found that IRS's methodology for counting returns did not include two categories of duplicate returns that should have been included in the estimates. IRS officials estimated that including these returns would increase IRS's original 2013 estimates of refunds paid out by $0.47 billion, from $4.75 billion to $5.22 billion in filing season 2013.

APPENDIX II: OBJECTIVES, SCOPE, AND METHODOLOGY

This report examines (1) what the Internal Revenue Service (IRS) knows about the extent of identity theft (IDT) refund fraud and (2) what additional actions IRS can take to combat IDT refund fraud using third-party information (for example, from employers and financial institutions). As described earlier, the report discusses IDT refund fraud and not employment fraud, unless otherwise noted.

To understand what IRS knows about the extent of IDT refund fraud, we reviewed IRS's *Identity Theft Taxonomy (Taxonomy)*, which estimates the amount of IDT refund fraud that IRS is, and is not, preventing. We conducted manual data testing for obvious errors and compared underlying data to IRS's *Refund Fraud & Identity Theft Global Report.* We confirmed *Taxonomy* components where we had data available to cross check. We also interviewed IRS officials to better understand the methodology used to create the estimates and the changes in methodology, data sources, and assumptions across the years of data available. For details on our findings about the *Taxonomy* components we evaluated, see appendix I.

To identify opportunities to improve IRS's IDT refund fraud efforts, we reviewed *Internal Revenue Manual* sections detailing IRS's Identity Protection Program and IRS documentation for its External Leads Program, the Opt-In Program, and other third-party efforts. We also reviewed Treasury's legislative proposals and Congressional testimony of IRS officials. We interviewed officials and reviewed documentation from the Social Security Administration (SSA) and several of the third parties shown in table 1 below, where applicable. We selected a nonprobability sample of 22 associations and stakeholders with differing positions and characteristics to help ensure our analysis covered a variety of viewpoints, based on IRS documentation and suggestions, our prior work, and other information. For example, to select associations representing financial institutions, we considered, among other factors, the size and type of institutions they represented (e.g., large or small banks, credit unions, and prepaid debit card companies). Because we used a nonprobability sample, the views of these associations are not generalizable to all potential third parties.

When possible, we used a standard set of questions in interviewing these associations and summarized the results of the semistructured interviews. However, as needed, we also sought perspectives on additional questions tailored to these associations' expertise and sought their opinions on key issues. We then discussed these options with officials from IRS offices, including (1) Privacy, Government Liaison, and Disclosure and (2) Return Integrity and Correspondence Services to determine the feasibility of various options and the challenges of pursuing them.

To describe the timing of refunds issued compared to W-2 submissions, we analyzed SSA data for filing season 2013 and IRS data for filing season 2012.[1] SSA provided data on the cumulative number of W-2s it received for filing season 2013. We assessed the reliability of SSA data by performing electronic tests to identify obvious errors and discussing the data with SSA officials. We found the data were sufficiently reliable for the purposes of providing contextual information on when SSA receives W-2s.

Table 1. List of Third Parties Interviewed

Software and Analytics Companies	1. Equifax 2. H&R Block[a] 3. Intuit 4. LexisNexis 5. SAS
Tax Software and Return Preparer Associations and Advisory Committees	6. American Coalition for Taxpayer Rights 7. American Institute of CPAs 8. Electronic Tax Administration Advisory Committee 9. Free File Alliance
Financial Institution and Payment Associations	10. American Bankers Association 11. BITS[b] 12. The Clearing House 13. Credit Union National Association[c] 14. NACHA – The Electronic Payments Association 15. National Association of Federal Credit Unions 16. Network Branded Prepaid Card Association
Payroll, Information Reporting, and Small Business Associations	17. American Payroll Association 18. Information Reporting Program Advisory Committee 19. National Federation of Independent Businesses 20. Reporting Agent Forum
Others	21. Federation of Tax Administrators 22. National Taxpayer Advocate

Source: GAO. | GAO-14-633.

[a] Also offers in-person tax preparation and banking services.

[b] Technology policy division of the Financial Services Roundtable. BITS is not an acronym. At one time, BITS stood for "Banking Industry Technology Secretariat." However, with financial modernization and the emergence of integrated financial services companies, that term is no longer used.

[c] Provided written comments.

For IRS data, we used analysis developed for GAO-13-515 on the timing of W-2s and tax returns. This analysis obtained data from IRS's Compliance Data Warehouse (CDW) database, which provides a variety of tax return, enforcement, compliance, and other data.[2] In analyzing when tax returns were received by IRS, we used the cycle posting date (when IRS posts tax return data to the master file), as it represents when the tax return data are available for matching. Officials noted that IRS must refine the data prior to posting to IRS systems. This may include identifying and correcting incomplete or inaccurate data before posting the data to IRS systems. We assessed the reliability of CDW data by (1) performing electronic or manual testing of required data elements to identify obvious errors, (2) reviewing existing information about the data and the system that produced them, and (3) interviewing agency officials knowledgeable about the data. We determined that the data were sufficiently reliable for the purposes of this report.

We conducted this performance audit from May 2014 to August 2014 in accordance with generally accepted government auditing standards. Those standards require that we plan and perform the audit to obtain sufficient, appropriate evidence to provide a reasonable basis for our findings and conclusions based on our audit objectives. We believe that the evidence obtained provides a reasonable basis for our findings and conclusions based on our audit objectives.

End Notes

[1] IRS, Strategic Plan: FY2014-2017, (Washington, D.C.: 2014).

[2] GAO, Identity Theft: Total Extent of Refund Fraud Using Stolen Identities is Unknown, GAO-13-132T (Washington, D.C.: Nov. 29, 2012).

[3] In certain instances, IRS requests W-2 information from employers to validate information on returns selected by fraud filters.

[4] Employers must provide W-2s to employees by January 31 and to SSA by February 29 (for paper W-2s) and March 31 (for e-filed W-2s).

[5] For 2014, IRS informed taxpayers that it would generally issue refunds in less than 21 days after receiving a tax return. IRS is required by law to pay interest if it takes longer than 45 days after the due date of the return to issue a refund. 26 U.S.C. § 6611(e).

[6] GAO, Tax Refunds: IRS is Exploring Verification Improvements, but Needs to Better Manage Risks, GAO-13-515 (Washington, D.C.: June 4, 2013).

[7] If a subsequent return using the SSN is filed on paper, IRS systems detect the return during processing.

[8] Two of the tax-administration systems employing filters are the Dependent Database (DDb) and Electronic Fraud Detection System (EFDS). DDb incorporates IRS, Health & Human Services, and Social Security Administration data to identify compliance issues involving IDT, refundable credits, and prisoners. EFDS is a legacy system built in the mid-1990s. To replace EFDS, IRS is developing the Return Review Program.

[9] GAO, Standards for Internal Control in the Federal Government, GAO/AIMD-00-21.3.1 (Washington, D.C.: Nov. 1, 1999).

[10] During the course of our audit, we found that IRS's methodology for counting returns did not include two categories of duplicate returns that should have been included in the estimates. IRS officials estimated that including these returns would increase IRS's original 2013 estimates of refunds paid out by $0.47 billion, from $4.75 billion to $5.22 billion in filing season 2013.

[11] See appendix I for additional details on limitations.

[12] GAO, Improper Payments: Remaining Challenges and Strategies for Governmentwide Reduction Efforts, GAO-12-573T (Washington, D.C.: Mar. 28, 2012).

[13] RRP is intended to be a web-based automated system designed to enhance IRS's capabilities to detect, resolve, and prevent criminal and civil noncompliance. While IRS recently launched an initial version of RRP to run parallel with EFDS, IRS officials told us that the next version is on a "strategic pause" while IRS officials clarify RRP's functionality.

[14] Currently, employers who file 250 or more W-2s annually must e-file those forms. 26 C.F.R. § 301.6011-2(b)(2). IRS is generally prohibited from requiring those filing fewer than 250 returns annually to e-file. 26 U.S.C. § 6011(e)(2)(A).

[15] We used analysis from GAO-13-515, which included data on the timing of W-2s and tax returns. SSA transmits wage data to IRS immediately upon receiving electronic W-2s, according to SSA officials. Paper W-2s require manual handling and therefore have a significantly longer processing time.

[16] 26 U.S.C. § 6611(e).

[17] Estimated based on 99 percent of all refund returns.

[18] Treasury, General Explanations of the Administration's Fiscal Year 2015 Revenue Proposals, (Washington, D.C.: Mar. 2014). Each February, Treasury releases this publication in conjunction with the President's budget. As part of its proposal to stagger tax return filing dates, Treasury proposed implementing an accelerated deadline for filing information returns and eliminating the extended due date for e-filed returns. Under the proposal, paper and e-filed W-2s would be due to SSA by January 31, the same date W-2s are due to employees.

[19] IRS, Fiscal Year 2015 President's Budget, (Washington, D.C.). IRS requested $21.6 million and 51 full time equivalents to fund five information technology projects, including a project to improve access to SSA data.

[20] John Koskinen, Commissioner of Internal Revenue, oral testimony before the Senate Appropriations Subcommittee on Financial Services and General Government, 113th Cong., Apr. 30, 2014.

[21] See, for example, National Taxpayer Advocate, 2013 Annual Report to Congress, Vol. II: (Washington, D.C.: Dec. 31, 2013).

[22] While IRS could conduct pre-refund matching using other types of information returns (such as Forms 1099), we focus on W-2s in this report because IRS officials and third parties we spoke with discussed the Form W-2 as a specific tool for combating IDT refund fraud.

[23] According to IRS officials, under the current pre-refund process, IRS only uses employer-reported W-2 data to verify information on returns selected by fraud filters (about 1 percent of all returns IRS receives). To perform these verification checks, IRS contacts individual employers to verify wage and withholding information.

[24] Employers file Form W-2c, Corrected Wage and Tax Statements (W-2c), when they need to make changes to previously submitted W-2s. For example, employers may file W2cs to correct errors reported by employees.

[25] National Payroll Reporting Consortium, Inc. (NPRC), Internal Revenue Service Public Hearing: Proposed Real-Time Tax System, (Washington, D.C.: Jan. 25, 2012). To provide

information about the potential volume of corrected W-2s arising from an earlier deadline, NPRC analyzed payroll firm data on client submissions at the end of each quarter and subsequent adjustments submitted after the cutoff dates. NPRC did not analyze the impact of a January 31 deadline but based on this analysis, an NPRC official indicated a January 31 deadline would not dramatically increase corrections from current levels.

[26] Employers must submit W-2 forms to employees by January 31 and to SSA by February 29 (if filing on paper) and March 31 (if e-filing).

[27] SSA provided weekly data on W-2s. April 5, 2013 was the Friday following the March 31, 2013 deadline for e-filing W-2s.

[28] IRS, Strategic Plan: FY2014-2017.

[29] GAO/AIMD-00-21.3.1.

[30] 26 C.F.R. § 301.6011-2(b)(2). IRS is generally prohibited from requiring those filing fewer than 250 returns annually to e-file. 26 U.S.C. § 6011(e)(2)(A).

[31] According to 2011 U.S. Census Bureau data.

[32] American Payroll Association, PayState Update, vol. 16, iss. 2 (2014). Thresholds vary by state. For example, Connecticut and Virginia mandate e-filing for all employers. Other states require e-filing for more than 11-100 information returns.

[33] The third association did not comment on the e-file threshold during our interview.

[34] IRS made similar gradual threshold reductions when implementing e-filing requirements for paid preparers.

[35] We did not verify SSA's estimates.

[36] Treasury, General Explanations of the Administration's Fiscal Year 2015 Revenue Proposals.

[37] IRS, Strategic Plan: FY2014-2017.

[38] GAO/AIMD-00-21.3.1.

[39] Currently, IRS delays refunds for suspicious returns. For example, IRS's Taxpayer Protection Program reviews suspicious returns flagged by IRS's identity theft filters and requires taxpayers to confirm their identities before IRS issues the refund.

[40] The start of the filing season is typically in mid January, although IRS has delayed the start date of the filing season in the past, such as in 2013 and 2014.

[41] In our semistructured interviews, we did not specifically ask all 22 groups about the options of delaying refunds or delaying the filing season. Ten groups discussed delaying refunds or the filing season as a potential way for IRS to combat IDT refund fraud.

[42] National Taxpayer Advocate, 2013 Annual Report to Congress, Vol. II.

[43] IRS has a legal obligation to pay interest on refunds issued after 45 days from the due date of the tax return, and this requirement would apply to refund delays associated with pre-refund matching and IDT refund fraud detection. Taxpayers who currently receive their refunds prior to the 45-day deadline may incur opportunity costs to the extent they would not be able to accrue interest on the refund during the time period between the date they currently receive their refund and the 45-day deadline.

[44] According to IRS officials, IRS has received many suggestions from third parties. When deciding whether to implement these suggestions, officials consider factors such as budget, operational, and administrative constraints.

[45] IRS does not distinguish between leads based on suspicion of IDT refund fraud or other types of fraud.

[46] IRS, Strategic Plan: FY2014-2017.

[47] GAO/AIMD-00-21.3.1.

[48] Tax returns and other information submitted to and, in some cases, generated by IRS, are confidential and protected from disclosure, except as specifically authorized by statute. 26

U.S.C. § 6103. Section 6103 protections apply equally to all tax returns and tax information that IRS receives, and it has no exceptions for fraudulent returns. In instances where a fraudulent return is under investigation, section 6103 allows IRS to share the minimum amount of tax return information necessary with financial institutions to facilitate the return of a fraudulent refund to IRS. In cases where financial institutions have rejected direct deposit refunds as part of the Opt-In Program, section 6103 does not allow IRS to share specific tax information with the financial institution.

[49] For leads submitted by financial institutions through the External Leads Program, IRS contacts the institutions to request that a suspicious refund be returned to IRS, thereby indicating some information about whether the lead helped to identify fraud. In contrast, IRS cannot provide similar feedback to financial institutions participating in the Opt-In Program because of legal restrictions.

[50] In our semistructured interviews, we asked an open question about the extent to which IRS provided feedback. The five groups volunteered this particular impact.

[51] According to a BITS official, the Financial Services Roundtable represents the largest integrated financial services companies providing banking, insurance payment and investment products and services to the American consumer. BITS addresses emerging technology and operational opportunities for the financial services industry, helping members manage risk, particularly in cybersecurity, fraud reduction, vendor management, and critical infrastructure protection. BITS is not an acronym. At one time, BITS stood for "Banking Industry Technology Secretariat." However, with financial modernization and the emergence of integrated financial services companies, that term is no longer used.

[52] According to a BITS official, this information is available upon request through BITS for any financial institutions that are not its members. However, financial institutions need to know this information is available through BITS in order to request it.

[53] GAO, Managing for Results: Enhancing Agency Use of Performance Information for Management Decision Making, GAO-05-927 (Washington, D.C.: Sept. 9, 2005).

[54] IRS, Strategic Plan: FY2014-2017, (Washington, D.C.: 2014).

[55] GAO, Internal Revenue Service: Absorbing Budget Cuts Has Resulted in Significant Staffing Declines and Uneven Budget Performance, GAO-14-534R (Washington, D.C.: Apr. 21, 2014).

End Notes for Appendix II

[1] Our analysis of IRS data on the timing of information returns is from a previous report (GAO-13-515).

[2] Our analysis of IRS data is based on return data extracted from CDW April 17, 2013. For our previous review, IRS officials reviewed our information return counts as of this date and confirmed that our data were substantially the same as their counts at that time.

In: Identity Theft Tax Refund Fraud   ISBN: 978-1-63482-602-0
Editor: Lucas Haynes   © 2015 Nova Science Publishers, Inc.

Chapter 2

IDENTITY THEFT AND TAX FRAUD: ENHANCED AUTHENTICATION COULD COMBAT REFUND FRAUD, BUT IRS LACKS AN ESTIMATE OF COSTS, BENEFITS AND RISKS[*]

United States Government Accountability Office

WHY GAO DID THIS STUDY

IRS estimated it prevented $24.2 billion in fraudulent identity theft (IDT) refunds in 2013, but paid $5.8 billion later determined to be fraud. Because of the difficulties in knowing the amount of undetected fraud, the actual amount could differ from these point estimates. IDT refund fraud occurs when an identity thief uses a legitimate taxpayer's identifying information to file a fraudulent tax return and claims a refund.

GAO was asked to review IRS's efforts to combat IDT refund fraud. This report, the second in a series, assesses (1) the quality of IRS's IDT refund fraud cost estimates, and (2) IRS's progress in developing processes to enhance taxpayer authentication.

---

[*] This is an edited, reformatted and augmented version of a United States Government Accountability Office publication, No. GAO-15-119, dated January 2015.

GAO compared IRS's IDT estimate methodology to *GAO Cost Guide* best practices (fraud is a cost to taxpayers). To assess IRS's progress enhancing authentication, GAO reviewed IRS documentation and interviewed IRS officials, other government officials, and associations representing software companies, return preparers, and financial institutions.

WHAT GAO RECOMMENDS

GAO recommends IRS improve its fraud estimates by (1) reporting the inherent imprecision and uncertainty of estimates, and (2) documenting the underlying analysis justifying cost-influencing assumptions. In addition, IRS should estimate and document the economic costs, benefits and risks of possible options for taxpayer authentication. IRS agreed with GAO's recommendations and provided technical comments that GAO incorporated, as appropriate.

WHAT GAO FOUND

Identity Theft (IDT) Refund Fraud Cost Estimates

The Internal Revenue Service's (IRS) fraud estimates met several *GAO Cost Guide* best practices, such as documenting data sources and detailing calculations. However, the estimates do not reflect the uncertainty inherent in measuring IDT refund fraud because they are presented as point estimates. Best practices suggest that agencies assess the effects of assumptions and potential errors on estimates. Officials said they did not assess the estimates' level of uncertainty because of resource constraints and methodological challenges. Because making different assumptions could affect IDT fraud estimates by billions of dollars, a point estimate (as opposed to, for example, a range) could lead to different decisions about allocating IDT resources. Reporting the uncertainty that is already known from IRS analysis (and conducting further analyses when not cost prohibitive) might help IRS communicate IDT refund fraud's inherent complexity.

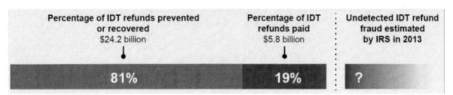

Percentage of IDT refunds prevented or recovered $24.2 billion	Percentage of IDT refunds paid $5.8 billion	Undetected IDT refund fraud estimated by IRS in 2013
81%	19%	?

Source: GAO analysis of IRS data. I   GAO-15-119.

IRS Estimates of Attempted IDT Refund Fraud, 2013.

While IRS's fraud estimates note the relevant cost assumptions used to develop estimates, they do not provide the rationale or analysis to support them. Officials stated they did not document the rationale because of the time and resources required. Best practices suggest that agencies should document assumptions. Given the evolving nature of IDT refund fraud, documenting assumptions' rationale would help IRS management and policymakers determine whether the assumptions remain valid or need to be updated.

Taxpayer Authentication

IRS recently created a group aimed at centralizing several prior ad hoc efforts to authenticate taxpayers across its systems. IRS's planning documentation contains goals and short- and long-term priorities (including implementation plans). However, a commitment to cost, benefit and risk analysis is not documented in the group's short- and long-term priorities. The draft planning documentation makes no mention of where such analyses would be included in IRS's priorities. Office of Management and Budget guidance states that agencies should use cost-benefit analyses that consider alternatives to promote efficient resource allocation and that agencies should ensure that authentication processes provide the appropriate level of assurance by assessing risks. Without analysis of costs, benefits and risks, IRS and Congress will not have quantitative information that could inform decisions about whether and how much to invest in the various authentication options. Cost, benefit and risk estimates for authentication would have the additional benefit of allowing comparisons with other options for combating IDT refund fraud. IDT options could have significant costs for taxpayers and IRS, so more information about the tradeoffs would help inform IRS and congressional decision making.

ABBREVIATIONS

AGI	adjusted gross income
AUR	Automated Underreporter
DDb	Dependent Database
EFDS	Electronic Fraud Detection System
e-file	electronically file
GAO Cost Guide	*GAO Cost Estimating and Assessment Guide*
Global Report	*Refund Fraud and Identity Theft Global Report*
IDT	identity theft
IP PIN	Identity Protection Personal Identification Number
IRS	Internal Revenue Service
NIST	National Institute of Standards and Technology
NSTIC	National Strategy for Trusted Identities in Cyberspace
OMB	Office of Management and Budget
PIN	Personal Identification Number
RRP	Return Review Program
SSN	Social Security number
Taxonomy	IRS *Identity Theft Taxonomy*
Treasury	Department of the Treasury
W-2	Form W-2, *Wage and Tax Statement*

* * *

January 20, 2015
The Honorable Orrin Hatch
United States Senate

The Honorable Ron Wyden
United States Senate

The Honorable Susan M. Collins
United States Senate

The Honorable Bill Nelson
United States Senate

The Honorable Paul Ryan
House of Representatives

Tax refund fraud associated with identity theft (IDT) is a complex and rapidly changing threat facing the nation's tax system. IDT refund fraud occurs when a refund-seeking identity thief obtains an individual's identifying information and uses it to file a fraudulent tax return.[1] IDT refund fraud burdens honest taxpayers who have had fraudulent tax returns filed in their name because they must deal with delayed refunds as they authenticate their identities with the Internal Revenue Service (IRS). Additionally, IDT refund fraud is an attractive target for criminals with a potentially high payoff. While the estimates have inherent uncertainty, IRS estimated that it prevented $24.2 billion in fraudulent IDT refunds in filing season 2013. However, IRS also estimated, where data were available, that it paid $5.8 billion in fraudulent IDT refunds.[2] Because of the difficulties in knowing the amount of undetected fraud, the actual amount could differ from these point estimates.[3]

This is the second in a series of our reports on IDT refund fraud. In August 2014, we issued a report describing what IRS knew about the extent of IDT refund fraud and identifying additional actions IRS could take to combat IDT refund fraud using third-party information.[4] One action that the first report focused on was matching wage information that IRS receives from employers (on Form W-2, *Wage and Tax Statement* (W-2)) to tax returns before issuing refunds. While there is no "silver bullet" for combating IDT refund fraud, IRS officials told us that pre-refund W-2 matching could prevent billions of dollars in estimated IDT refund fraud; however, pre-refund matching would have costs. We noted that pre-refund W-2 matching would likely require some combination of accelerated due dates for information returns, delayed start of the annual tax filing season, delayed refund issuance, and investments in IRS information systems with the capability of doing real-time matching. We found that IRS had not considered how to implement such changes, including identifying their costs and benefits. We recommended that the agency estimate the costs and benefits to inform a discussion about whether to proceed. In November 2014, IRS reported that it had convened an internal working group to address our recommendations and that it anticipated implementing our recommendations by July 2015.

IRS has other pre-refund options for preventing IDT refund fraud. Two options that the agency is exploring are (1) tracking device identification numbers to determine when multiple returns are filed from the same device (e.g., the same laptop computer), and (2) authenticating the identity of a taxpayer before issuing a refund through the use of security questions, passwords, and other techniques.[5]

Within this context, you asked us to continue examining IRS's efforts to combat IDT refund fraud. This report assesses (1) the quality of the IRS *Identity Theft Taxonomy's* (*Taxonomy*) estimates of the cost of IDT refund fraud, and (2) IRS's progress in developing processes to track device identification numbers and to enhance taxpayer authentication.[6]

To assess the quality of the *Taxonomy's* estimates of IDT-related refund fraud, we reviewed the *Taxonomy's* methodology for filing season 2013 and evaluated it against selected best practices in the *GAO Cost Estimating and Assessment Guide* that were applicable to the *Taxonomy* and consistent with IRS and Office of Management and Budget (OMB) information quality guidelines.[7] Appendix I explains our scope and methodology and provides a summary of best practices selected. These best practices are relevant because the *Taxonomy* is an estimate of the amount of revenue lost to IDT refund fraud—a cost to taxpayers. We discussed the criteria with IRS officials, who generally agreed with their applicability to the *Taxonomy*.[8] We conducted manual data testing for obvious errors and compared underlying data to IRS's *Refund Fraud & Identity Theft Global Report*. We also interviewed IRS officials to better understand the methodology IRS used to create the estimates.

To assess IRS's progress in developing processes to track device identification numbers and to enhance taxpayer authentication, we reviewed *Internal Revenue Manual* sections detailing IRS's Identity Protection Program, and IRS documentation for several tools developed to combat IDT refund fraud. These included the Identity Protection Personal Identification Number (IP PIN), device identification, and other efforts related to identity authentication. We compared IRS's authentication group's planning documentation to OMB's guidance on cost-benefit analyses, as well as OMB and National Institute for Standards and Technology (NIST) guidance on assessing levels of assurance for electronic authentication. [9] We also interviewed officials from NIST and associations representing software companies, return preparers, and financial institutions. To help ensure our analysis covered a variety of viewpoints, we selected a nonprobability sample of 18 associations and stakeholders with differing positions and characteristics based on IRS documentation and suggestions, our prior work, and other information. Because we used a nonprobability sample, the views of these associations are not generalizable to all potential third parties. We then communicated with IRS offices to determine the feasibility of various options and the challenges of pursuing them. See appendix I for details on our scope and methodology.

We conducted this performance audit from August 2013 to January 2015 in accordance with generally accepted government auditing standards. Those standards require that we plan and perform the audit to obtain sufficient, appropriate evidence to provide a reasonable basis for our findings and conclusions based on our audit objectives. We believe that the evidence obtained provides a reasonable basis for our findings and conclusions based on our audit objectives.

BACKGROUND

Identity Theft Refund Fraud – Key Components

IDT refund fraud occurs in the context of several inter-related issues: the vulnerability of personal information, thieves' ability to exploit IRS's current compliance model, and the attractiveness of IDT refund fraud as a target.

Theft of Personal Information

To successfully commit IDT refund fraud, thieves must exploit various sources of information to steal or otherwise obtain individuals' identities. According to an official in IRS's Criminal Investigation division, the sources of stolen identities are limitless. The Department of Justice has prosecuted cases ranging from an employee stealing information from his employer to organized cyber attacks that infiltrate computer systems.

Exploitation of IRS Compliance Checks

After obtaining personal information belonging to legitimate taxpayers (or to individuals who do not have a tax filing obligation), identity thieves use this information to file fraudulent tax returns claiming refunds. Identity thieves are often able to exploit what IRS officials call a "look back" compliance model: rather than holding refunds until all compliance checks can be completed, IRS issues refunds after doing some selected, automated reviews of taxpayer-submitted information (see text box). IRS is under pressure from taxpayers who expect to receive their refunds quickly.[10] As a result, IRS normally issues refunds before matching tax returns to third-party information returns (such as W-2 data).

Examples of automated reviews used
• Matching name and Social Security number (SSN) • Correcting obvious errors—such as mathematical mistakes or exceeding the statutory limits of deductions and credits.

Source: GAO analysis of IRS documents. | GAO-15-119.

Attractiveness of IDT Refund Fraud

IDT refund fraud crimes often involve large criminal enterprises that exploit the speed and relative anonymity of preparing and filing tax returns. For this reason, they are difficult to prosecute, according to the Department of Justice.

IRS's Current IDT Refund Fraud Response

In light of the complexity and fluidity of this threat, IRS addressed refund fraud and IDT in its strategic plan, identifying both issues as major challenges facing the nation's tax system over the next several years (see text box).[11]

IRS: Addressing the Threat of Refund Fraud and Identity Theft
"Assuring the accuracy of refunds and the security of taxpayer data remain our priorities going forward. We are committed to stopping this threat to tax administration, protecting our government's revenue and safeguarding the identity of all taxpayers. We must bolster our efforts to prevent refund fraud and identity theft before they happen."

Source: IRS Strategic Plan: FY2014-2017. | GAO-15-119.

The plan further states that IRS is committed to building a stronger identity authentication process that will enable secure, timely processing of tax returns and improve other service interactions. IRS has also identified several strategic objectives relevant to its efforts to combat identity theft, including

- balancing the speed of refund delivery with the need to verify taxpayers' identities; and
- using third-party data, risk modeling, and a historical view of taxpayer interactions to prevent fraud before issuing refunds.

Further, IRS has allocated more than 3,000 employees to combat IDT refund fraud, including assigning staff to help IDT victims resolve their accounts. The agency has also requested an additional $64.9 million in its fiscal year 2015 budget request for staffing and advanced technologies to support its continued IDT and refund fraud efforts.

In addition to identifying IDT refund fraud as a major issue and requesting additional resources, IRS has developed a number of tools to address IDT refund fraud throughout the tax return filing process—and has done so amidst budget reductions and other challenges.[12] IRS's response to IDT refund fraud includes efforts to authenticate taxpayer identities as well as several tools used to detect and prevent IDT refund fraud, as described below (see appendix II for more detail on these IDT refund fraud tools).

Authenticating Taxpayer Identities

IRS has enhanced its authentication efforts to combat IDT refund fraud. For example, IRS provides IP PINs to past IDT victims who have confirmed their identities with IRS. IP PINs help prevent future IDT refund fraud because, once issued, the IP PIN must accompany an electronically filed (e-file) tax return.[13] In addition, IRS conducts authentication checks on returns flagged by IDT and fraud filters. If flagged, IRS stops processing the return and sends a letter asking the taxpayer to confirm his or her identity. IRS then confirms the taxpayer's identity by asking for personal information, such as the taxpayer's previous addresses, mortgage lender, and family members.

Taxpayer Alerts

Often, IRS becomes aware of IDT refund fraud when a legitimate taxpayer alerts IRS of an inability to e-file. Specifically, in cases where an identity thief has already e-filed a return using the taxpayer's name and Taxpayer Identification Number—such as an SSN—IRS's e-file system will reject the second, duplicate return (top of figure 1), thus preventing the legitimate taxpayer from filing. IRS officials are aware when their e-file system rejects returns; however, they do not know if the rejections are due to IDT refund fraud unless further investigation is conducted.

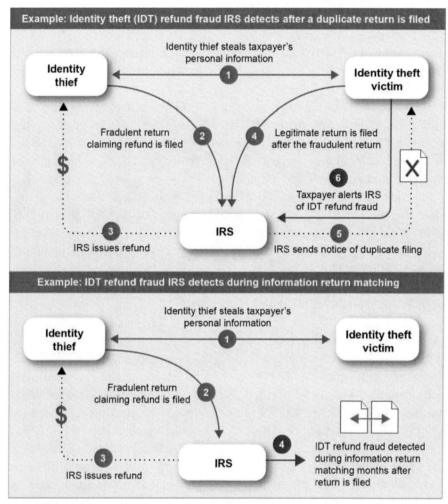

Source: GAO analysis of IRS documents. | GAO-15-119.
Note: In the examples, numbers represent the order in which these actions occur.
Examples in the graphic do not include instances where IRS detects IDT refund
fraud and prevents a refund.

Figure 1. Detecting IDT After Refunds are Issued: Two Examples.

Information Return Matching

IRS also finds IDT refund fraud as part of the Automated Underreporter
(AUR) program, which matches tax return data to information returns, such as
the W-2. These information returns are provided by third parties such as
employers, financial institutions, and others. In many cases, IRS does not

receive the information returns until well after the tax return and refund are processed (bottom of figure 1). In these types of cases, the legitimate taxpayer may not be aware of a stolen identity until after receiving a notice indicating that the income (or payment information) IRS has on file does not match the information reported on the tax return. We previously found that these post-refund compliance checks can take a year or more to complete, which can be a burden to taxpayers who receive a notice.[14] IRS officials acknowledge that the longer the delay between filing a tax return and receiving an IRS notice, the harder it can be for taxpayers to locate tax records or other information necessary to respond to IRS.

Fraud Filters

IRS also uses IDT and other fraud filters to detect IDT refund fraud. These filters are computerized automatic checks that screen returns using characteristics that IRS has identified in previous IDT refund fraud schemes. The filters also search for clusters of returns with similar characteristics, such as the same bank account or address, which could indicate potential fraud. Two of the tax-administration systems employing filters are the Dependent Database (DDb) and Electronic Fraud Detection System (EFDS). [15] IRS is also developing the Return Review Program (RRP) to replace EFDS. In April 2014, IRS began a pilot of one of RRP's planned fraud detection capabilities focused on detecting IDT refund fraud (e.g., RRP's IDT model).[16] IRS officials said that they plan to use RRP's IDT model on all returns in filing season 2015. Returns flagged by the RRP IDT model will go through the same process as returns flagged by other filters (as previously described).

IRS's Efforts to Identify and Monitor the Extent of IDT Refund Fraud

According to IRS officials, a vital component in the agency's strategy to identify IDT refund fraud is its *Identity Theft Taxonomy (Taxonomy)*. This research-based effort has several objectives, including (1) providing information to internal and external stakeholders about the effectiveness of IRS's IDT defenses, (2) helping IRS identify IDT trends and evolving risks, and (3) refining IDT filters to better detect potentially fraudulent returns while reducing the likelihood of flagging legitimate tax returns.

Taxonomy Methodology

Consisting of a matrix of IDT refund fraud categories (see figure 2), IRS's *Taxonomy* estimates the number of identified IDT refund fraud cases where IRS (1) prevented or recovered the fraudulent refunds (turquoise band), and (2) paid the fraudulent refunds (purple band). IRS breaks these estimates into six categories associated with IDT detection strategies. These strategies occur at three key points in the life cycle of a tax refund: before accepting a tax return, during return processing, and post refund.

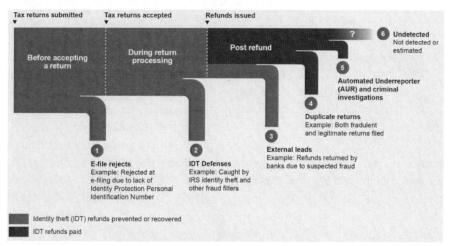

Source: GAO analysis of *IRS Taxonomy*. | GAO-15-119.

Figure 2. Illustration of IRS *Identity Theft Taxonomy*.

Taxonomy Categories

Estimates in categories 1-3 are based on IRS's *Refund Fraud & Identity Theft Global Report (Global Report)*, which consolidates IRS administrative records of known IDT refund fraud.[17] Category 4 estimates are based on duplicate returns, where IRS has received both a fraudulent IDT return and a legitimate return. Category 5 estimates are based on cases identified as part of a criminal investigation or as part of the AUR program. To estimate the AUR portion of category 5, IRS developed assumptions based on its analysis of the characteristics of past IDT refund fraud; IRS then used these assumptions to identify which information return mismatches were likely IDT returns.[18] Category 6 represents undetected IDT returns.

Current Taxonomy Estimates

Based upon its *Taxonomy*, IRS estimated that $30 billion in IDT refund fraud was attempted in filing season 2013 (see figure 3). Of this attempted amount of IDT refund fraud, IRS estimated that it prevented or recovered $24.2 billion (81 percent) of the estimated total. IRS also estimated it paid $5.8 billion (19 percent) in IDT refunds on 1 million IDT returns during the same time frame.[19] *Taxonomy* estimates do not include the amount of IDT refund fraud from schemes IRS cannot detect (e.g., schemes that involve reported income that IRS cannot confirm during information return matching).

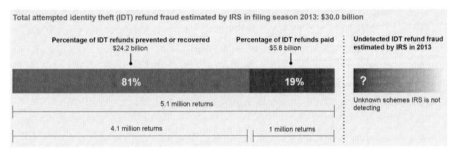

Source: GAO analysis of IRS data. | GAO-15-119.

Figure 3. Updated IRS *Taxonomy* Estimates of Attempted Identity Theft Refund Fraud, Filing Season 2013.

Administration Prioritizes Identity Theft and Authentication Efforts

In October 2014, the administration announced a plan to combat identity theft and further strengthen the security of personal identifying information maintained by the government.[20] The plan is intended to ensure that all agencies making personal data accessible to citizens online will require the use of multiple authentication steps and will have an effective identity proofing process. National Security Council staff, the Office of Science and Technology Policy, and the Office of Management and Budget (OMB) are tasked with developing this plan by January 2015, and relevant agencies shall complete any required implementation steps set forth in this plan by April 2016. Therefore, while this plan may aid IRS in its efforts to prevent identity theft, any implementation of the plan at the agency level is still a few years away.

TAXONOMY MET SEVERAL BEST PRACTICES FOR COST ESTIMATING, BUT IT COULD BETTER EXPLAIN ASSUMPTIONS AND REFLECT INHERENT UNCERTAINTY

Taxonomy Documented Data and Methodology

By providing insight into how IDT refund fraud is evading IRS defenses, estimates inform IRS decision making about how to improve fraud filters and other detection efforts. Objective estimates may also inform congressional decision making about IRS resources. To ensure that IRS information reporting is objective, the agency developed information quality guidelines.[21] Objectivity involves ensuring that information is reliable, accurate, and unbiased, as defined in OMB information quality guidelines.[22] Further, OMB quality guidelines state that, where appropriate, supporting data should include full, accurate, transparent documentation, and should disclose error sources affecting data quality.

We evaluated *Taxonomy* estimates against selected *GAO Cost Estimating and Assessment Guide (GAO Cost Guide)* best practices that (1) are related to OMB's definition of objectivity, and (2) are applicable to the *Taxonomy*. [23] These best practices are intended to ensure the reliability of estimates—a key component of OMB's definition of objectivity. While IRS is not required to follow the *GAO Cost Guide* best practices, following such practices could help the agency meet OMB and IRS information quality guidelines and could improve the reliability of IDT refund fraud estimates. We assessed the extent to which IRS provided evidence that the *Taxonomy* met each best practice and assigned ratings based on a five-point scale (Met, Substantially met, Partially met, Minimally met, or Not met). See appendix I for details on how we conducted our assessment.

As shown in table 1, the *Taxonomy* met several *GAO Cost Guide* best practices. IRS documented the *Taxonomy*'s source data, identified the methodology used to develop the estimate, and described how the estimate was developed. With regard to the calculation of *Taxonomy* estimates, our data reliability testing did not find calculation errors or other mistakes.[24]

Table 1. Summary of GAO's Assessment of *Taxonomy* Estimates Using the *GAO Cost Guide*, Filing Season 2013

Best practice characteristics	Assessment of whether best practices are met
Captures the source data used.	The *Taxonomy* documentation captures the source data used. *(Met)*
Describes in sufficient detail the calculations performed and the estimating methodology used to derive each element's cost.	The *Taxonomy* documentation describes in detail the calculations performed and the methodology used to derive each *Taxonomy* category. *(Met)*
Describes step by step how the estimate was developed so that a cost analyst unfamiliar with the program could understand what was done and replicate it.	The *Taxonomy* documentation describes step by step how the estimate was developed. *(Met)*
Contains few mistakes.	Our data reliability testing did not find calculation errors or other mistakes.a *(Met)*
Is regularly updated to reflect significant changes in the methodology.	IRS officials regularly update the *Taxonomy* methodology to better reflect evolving IDT refund fraud schemes and to improve the accuracy of *Taxonomy* estimates. *(Met)*
Includes all relevant costs.	The filing season 2013 *Taxonomy* estimates the number of cases of IDT refund fraud and associated costs throughout the life cycle of a tax return. Methodology improvements made filing season 2013 estimates more comprehensive by including categories of IDT returns that had not been included in filing season 2012 estimates. However, IRS has been unable to estimate the amount of IDT refund fraud from undetected schemes, such as when there is no information reporting to verify income. While IRS has considered a different approach to estimating the costs of undetected IDT, administrative costs and taxpayer burden are likely to make these approaches impractical. *(Partially met)*
Provides evidence that the cost estimate was reviewed and accepted by management.	The *Taxonomy* documentation does not provide evidence that the cost estimate was reviewed and accepted by management. However, IRS officials stated they are working on a new process to document management review and approval. *(Partially met)*

Table 1. (Continued)

Best practice characteristics	Assessment of whether best practices are met
Documents all cost-influencing ground rules and assumptions.	The *Taxonomy* documentation notes the assumptions used to develop the estimates. However, it does not provide the rationale or analysis supporting those assumptions. The assumptions likely result in overestimates for some categories and underestimates for others; however, methodology and data limitations make it unlikely that IRS will be able to account for this in the short term, if ever. *(Partially met)*
Includes a sensitivity analysis.b	While IRS conducted a sensitivity analysis for one part of the *Taxonomy*, it did not conduct sensitivity analyses for other categories.*(Minimally met)*
Includes a risk and uncertainty analysis.c	The *Taxonomy* acknowledges that there is uncertainty in the estimates. For example, IRS documentation states that *Taxonomy* estimates for one category do not include fraud that IRS currently cannot detect (e.g., schemes that involve reported income that IRS cannot confirm during information return matching). However, because of methodology and resource constraints, IRS did not conduct a risk and uncertainty analysis that would have illustrated the cumulative effect that assumptions have on the cost estimate, according to IRS officials. *(Minimally met)*
Results are not overly conservative or optimistic, and are based on an assessment of most likely costs.	The *Taxonomy* documentation explicitly documents a key uncertainty in its estimates: IDT refund fraud that IRS currently does not detect. However, because IRS did not conduct risk and uncertainty analyses for the numerical estimates it did produce, the level of uncertainty associated with the estimates is unclear. Presenting the *Taxonomy* as a point estimate does not reflect the inherent uncertainty of the estimate. *(Minimally met)*

Source: GAO analysis of IRS *Identity Theft Taxonomy* documentation, interviews with IRS officials, and GAO-09-3SP. | GAO-15-119

Note: We determined the overall assessment rating by assigning the following ratings: Did not meet– IRS provided no evidence that satisfies any of the best practice; Minimally met–IRS provided evidence that satisfies a small portion of the best practice; Partially met–IRS provided evidence that satisfies about half of the best practice; Substantially met–IRS provided evidence that satisfies a large portion of the best practice; and Met–IRS provided complete evidence that satisfies the entire best practice. See appendix I for a description of how we conducted our assessment.

[a]There may be some types of error that our data reliability testing was unable to detect. For example, we cross-checked *Taxonomy* estimates against the *Global Report*; however, if the *Global Report* itself contains errors, our data reliability testing would not detect these errors.

[b]A sensitivity analysis (also known as "what if" analysis) examines the effect changing assumptions has on the estimate by changing one assumption at a time. It involves recalculating the estimate using differing assumptions to develop ranges of potential estimates.

[c]Risk and uncertainty analysis recognizes the potential for error and captures the cumulative effect that assumptions have on the cost estimate. It involves using methods to develop a range of costs around a point estimate.

Methodology Changes Increased Fraud Estimates by $1 Billion, and Officials are Developing a Process to Document Management Review

> **Cost Guide Best Practice:**
>
> - Is regularly updated to reflect significant changes in the methodology.
> - Includes all relevant costs.
> - Provides evidence that the cost estimate was reviewed and accepted by management.
>
> Source: GAO-09-3SP. | GAO-15-119

After initial development of the *Taxonomy* in 2013, IRS made methodology improvements that resulted in more comprehensive *Taxonomy* estimates. For example, the agency included categories of duplicate IDT returns that had not been in filing season 2012 estimates. IRS made these methodology changes to enable comparison across filing seasons in future years, and to respond to our data reliability questions, according to officials. As a result, 2013 filing season estimates of "IDT refunds paid" increased by about $1 billion from an original estimate of $4.8 billion to a revised estimate of $5.8 billion (see table 2 for details).

**Table 2. Changes in IRS *Identity Theft Taxonomy* Estimates of IDT
Refunds Paid, Filing Season 2013**

Date	Estimate of IDT refunds paid	Amount increased from prior estimate	Reason for change
May 23, 2014 (original estimate)	$4.8 billion	Not applicable	Not applicable
June 23, 2014	$5.2 billion	$0.4 billion	In response to our questions, IRS officials agreed that the *Taxonomy's* methodology for counting returns should have included two categories of duplicate returns. Including these categories resulted in an increase in the amount of IDT refunds paid. We reported this figure in GAO-14-633.
July 22, 2014	$5.8 billion	$0.6 billion	IRS officials said they updated the *Taxonomy's* methodology to account for corrections within AUR data and to create a standard way of reporting estimates from year to year.

Source: GAO analysis of IRS Identity Theft Taxonomy and interviews with IRS officials. | GAO-15-119.

IRS officials have considered using surveys to develop a more comprehensive estimate of unidentified IDT refund fraud, but have not been able to develop a survey method that would avoid significant taxpayer burden and administrative costs. Accordingly, while IRS has made several methodology changes and refinements to improve *Taxonomy* estimates, it is unlikely that IRS will be able to develop a completely comprehensive estimate, given potential administrative costs and other constraints.

While *Taxonomy* documentation does not provide evidence of managerial review, IRS officials stated that the former IRS Acting Commissioner reviewed and approved the *Taxonomy*. Officials told us they are working on a new process to document management review and approval.

Taxonomy Notes Relevant Cost Assumptions Used, but Does Not Provide the Rationale or Analysis Supporting the Assumptions

> **Cost Guide Best Practice:**
>
> • Documents all cost-influencing ground rules and assumptions.
>
> Source: GAO-09-3SP. | GAO-15-119.

Developing loss estimates of illicit activities is challenging because such activities are difficult to observe. For this reason, IRS makes various assumptions, including whether an information return mismatch is an IDT return.

Taxonomy documentation thoroughly details IRS's assumptions. For example, the *Taxonomy* describes the assumptions used to develop its "refund paid" estimates in category 5, which are based on AUR data (see figure 2).[25] This part of the *Taxonomy* accounts for $3.0 billion of the estimated $5.8 billion in IDT refunds paid by IRS. However, the *Taxonomy* documentation for the AUR category does not provide information on the analysis or rationale used to develop the assumptions of past IDT refund fraud characteristics (see appendix III for examples showing how IRS assumptions affect *Taxonomy* results).

Given the evolving nature of IDT refund fraud, documenting *Taxonomy* assumptions and the rationale used to develop the assumptions would help IRS management and policymakers to determine whether the assumptions remain valid or need to be revised or updated. IRS officials acknowledged they could have better documented their analysis and rationale for choosing assumptions. They stated that IRS did not document its rationale for selecting assumptions because of the time and resources required.

Taxonomy assumptions also result in overestimates in some categories and underestimates in others. For example, while IRS's estimate for refunds prevented includes e-file rejects that occurred due to an incorrect or missing Identity Protection Personal Identification Number (IP PIN) (see figure 2), legitimate taxpayers may also have their return rejected if they include an incorrect IP PIN, or forget to include an IP PIN on their tax return. In addition, the same return—regardless of whether the return is filed by a legitimate taxpayer or an identity thief—can be rejected multiple times, which would result in an over-count of IDT refunds prevented. Officials said they do not collect data that would allow them to break out the amount of e-file rejects due to IDT refund fraud. According to IRS officials, the costs of collecting these data may outweigh the benefits, as it would require major changes to IRS information technology systems.

Point Estimates Do Not Reflect the *Taxonomy's* Inherent Uncertainty

Cost Guide Best Practice:
• Includes a sensitivity analysis.   • Includes a risk and uncertainty analysis.   • Results are not overly conservative or optimistic, and are based on an assessment of most likely costs.
Source: GAO-09-3SP. | GAO-15-119

To gain a better understanding of the effects that changing assumptions had on its estimates, IRS conducted a sensitivity analysis for category 5 "IDT refunds paid" estimates (which are based on AUR data from filing season 2013).[26] That analysis shows that making different assumptions could affect the estimate of category 5 IDT refunds paid by billions of dollars in either direction (see appendix III, example 1). However, IRS does not report a range or some other indication of the results of the sensitivity analysis when reporting the $5.8 billion estimate for IDT refund fraud detected after refunds were issued. IRS officials stated that their goal in developing the *Taxonomy* was to achieve a level of precision that would allow them to assess the effectiveness of IRS IDT defenses. Nor did IRS conduct sensitivity analyses for the other *Taxonomy* categories that include assumptions. Our analysis, shown in example 2 in appendix III, demonstrates that changes in these assumptions could affect estimates by billions of dollars. Also, IRS did not conduct a risk and uncertainty analysis showing the cumulative effect that assumptions have on the fraud estimate.27 As a result, the level of uncertainty associated with the *Taxonomy* estimates is unclear and users of the estimates may be left with a mistaken impression of their precision.

IRS officials stated that they did not conduct such analyses because of resource constraints and methodological challenges. Specifically, IRS officials stated that it would be methodologically difficult—if not impossible—to calculate uncertainty surrounding category 5 estimates that are based on AUR data. However, officials acknowledged that these analyses are possible for other categories in the *Taxonomy*, such as categories that use average refund value assumptions, or assumptions about the percent of returns detected by IRS defenses that are IDT.[28]

We recognize that conducting an uncertainty analysis will be challenging and add some costs; however, better reporting of what is already known from sensitivity analyses would not be costly. Reporting the uncertainty that is known already, and conducting further sensitivity analyses when not cost prohibitive, might help IRS communicate the complexities inherent in combating the evolving threat of IDT refund fraud. Reporting uncertainty, quantitatively if possible and otherwise qualitatively, could also give decision makers in Congress and IRS a more accurate understanding of what is known and not known about the extent of the IDT refund fraud problem. A point estimate, compared to a range or some other indication of uncertainty, could provide a false sense of precision leading to different decisions about how to allocate resources to combat IDT refund fraud.

Given methodological and resource constraints, there are various ways IRS could report the uncertainty in the IDT refund fraud estimates. One way would be to present a point estimate surrounded by quantitative estimates of the possible range. Another way would be to qualitatively describe the relative size of the uncertainty and the reasons for this uncertainty. For example, IRS could describe how changes in assumptions affect the *Taxonomy's* minimum, point, and maximum estimates.

IRS IS BEGINNING TO IMPLEMENT ONE NEW PRE-REFUND TOOL AND IS EXPLORING ENHANCED TAXPAYER AUTHENTICATION, BUT LACKS INFORMATION ON COSTS, BENEFITS AND RISKS

While it is likely that no one tool will stop all attempts at fraud, we have found that implementing strong preventive controls can help defend against invalid refunds, increasing public confidence and avoiding the difficult "pay and chase" aspects of recovering invalid refunds.[29] Recapturing a fraudulent refund after it is issued can be challenging—if not impossible—because identity thieves often spend or transfer the funds immediately, making them very difficult to trace. For this reason, IRS is in various stages of exploring several possible pre-refund tools. Three tools with significant potential are (1) pre-refund Form W-2, *Wage and Tax Statement* (W-2) matching (which we already noted was the subject of our August 2014 report), (2) device identification, and (3) improved taxpayer authentication.

IRS is Working with Tax Software Companies to Implement Device Identification

Based on suggestions from the tax software industry and internal stakeholders, IRS is beginning to implement device identification that would capture the unique number associated with the individual device, such as a laptop computer, used to e-file a return. IRS could use this information to determine when multiple fraudulent returns are filed from the same device.

In November 2014, IRS published guidance for e-file providers that outlined IRS's plans to collect device identification numbers along with tax returns for filing season 2015.[30] IRS officials told us they will collect device identification numbers voluntarily for this first year. Beginning in filing season 2016, IRS plans to require these companies to submit a device identification number with each e-filed tax return.[31]

From a cost-benefit perspective, IRS's implementation of device identification appears justified. One important benefit of device identification is that it will enhance IRS's ability to monitor when multiple returns are filed from the same device or from devices previously associated with fraud. In addition, device identification analysis could aid in criminal investigations, according to officials from one software industry group we interviewed.

Device identification will impose minimal, if any, costs on taxpayers, third parties, or IRS. It will not require additional taxpayer action, according to IRS. In addition, IRS and tax software companies told us that while tax software companies already capture device identification numbers when a taxpayer is preparing a return, that information is not currently transmitted to IRS. In contrast to some other options IRS is considering, such as earlier W-2 matching, IRS can use current information technology systems and processes to implement the device identification tool. For example, the device identification number will be transmitted to IRS via existing return transmission processes for e-filed returns. IRS could also use its existing filters as a low-cost method of determining patterns of device usage.

IRS is Pursuing Improved Taxpayer Authentication to Prevent IDT Refund Fraud; However, the Agency Does Not Have a Plan to Assess Costs, Benefits and Risks

IRS's Current Authentication Tools Have Limitations

IRS has developed various personal identification numbers (PIN) to authenticate taxpayers' identities and help verify the legitimacy of tax returns (see text box). Typically, these PINs are used by taxpayers to sign e-filed tax returns. IRS programs its systems to not accept a tax return if a required PIN is missing or does not match agency records. However, according to our analysis of IRS information and interviews with experts from tax software companies and associations, IRS's current authentication tools (such as the e-file PIN) have limitations.

PINs and the Identity Authentication They Require

- *Self-select PIN* – Most taxpayers are eligible to use the Self-Select PIN. The Self-Select PIN requires taxpayers to provide their prior year's adjusted gross income (AGI) amount or prior year's self created PIN to authenticate the taxpayer's identity.
- *E-file PIN* – If taxpayers do not have a self-select PIN or their prior year's AGI, they can obtain an e-file PIN. The e-file PIN requires taxpayers to authenticate their name, SSN, date of birth, address, and filing status.
- *IP PIN* – IRS provides IP PINs to past IDT victims who have confirmed their identities with IRS, or to taxpayers who participated in a pilot program. In filing season 2014, IRS offered this pilot to taxpayers in Florida, Georgia, and the District of Columbia.

Source: GAO analysis of IRS documents. | GAO-15-119.

- **Identity thieves may be able to falsely obtain e-file PINs.** Identity thieves can easily find the information needed to obtain an e-file PIN, allowing them to bypass some, if not all of IRS's current automatic checks, according to our analysis and interviews with tax software and return preparer associations and companies.[32] According to IRS, identity thieves can find identifying information through public records or other easily accessible sources.

- **Only a small number of taxpayers undergo knowledge-based authentication or receive IP PINs.** Knowledge-based authentication—a more intensive authentication process—uses questions about personal information that only the taxpayer should know to confirm taxpayers' identities. [33] Examples of authentication questions are "Who is your mortgage lender?" or "Which of the following is your previous address?" IRS uses authentication questions to confirm the identities of taxpayers whose returns are flagged by IRS's IDT and other fraud filters.[34] Only a limited number of returns—about 1 percent—are currently subject to this more intensive authentication process. IRS also uses authentication questions to confirm the identities of taxpayers who request an IP PIN. Because IRS did not advertise the IP PIN pilot, the participation rate for the pilot was low. According to IRS officials, as of July 31, 2014, IRS had received about 21,000 requests out of about 13.9 million eligible taxpayers (or about 0.15 percent of eligible taxpayers), in 2014. IDT thieves can also obtain and use credit bureau information to answer the authentication questions, according to IRS officials.

IRS Has Options for Improving Its Authentication Tools

IRS officials and several third parties, including software providers and paid preparers, suggested IRS could enhance its taxpayer authentication approach by expanding some current tools and by exploring additional options. According to our review of IRS and third-party information, each of these options has strengths and weaknesses. Unlike the device identification tool, these options could require substantial changes to tax administration and may burden taxpayers by requiring individuals to track additional information or to take additional steps when filing a tax return. Similar to pre-refund W-2 matching, improved authentication tools could provide substantial benefits but require major investments in IRS systems and changes to work processes. One advantage of authentication is that it could be applicable to more tax returns than pre-refund W-2 matching, since W-2 matching only works for tax returns reporting wage income. Authentication options include:

- **Expanding the use of current authentication questions to a wider set of taxpayers.** IRS could use authentication questions for the entire individual taxpayer population or in conjunction with other tools. IRS is continually analyzing the effectiveness of its authentication questions, which may be a benefit if the program was expanded. However, IRS analysis of single filers whose returns were flagged by fraud filters and who answered authentication questions has shown limitations: some likely identity thieves were able to correctly answer authentication questions while some legitimate taxpayers were not.[35]

- **Expanding the availability of the IP PIN pilot to additional taxpayers.** Currently, IP PIN distribution is limited to individuals who are IDT refund fraud victims or who participated in the IP PIN pilot. However, IRS is considering an expansion of the IP PIN to include more taxpayers. In responding to an open-ended question, 3 of the 18 associations we interviewed also suggested expanding the IP PIN pilot to all taxpayers as an optional effort.[36] An IP PIN provides an additional layer of security for taxpayers, according to IRS. However, the effectiveness of the IP PIN relies on the strength of authentication questions, which have the limitations described above. In addition, because taxpayers only use the IP PIN once a year when filing their returns, retrieving lost IP PINs creates additional burden for taxpayers and IRS.

- **Developing and issuing IRS or third-party credentials (e.g., username and password or tokens that generate random numbers) to taxpayers.** Under a credential system, taxpayers could actively confirm their identities through authentication questions and then receive a credential from IRS or a third party. [37] This credential could be required when filing taxes, and could also be used for other transactions. A study prepared for the National Institute for Standards and Technology (NIST) describes options for a credential system: an IRS-issued credential for filing taxes or a third-party-issued credential that could be used for other purposes (e.g., accessing an online bank account).[38] NIST found that improved authentication through a credential may help IRS more effectively combat IDT refund fraud, as it may allow IRS to target resources toward returns filed without a credential. However, obtaining a credential would involve some taxpayer burden. In addition, like the IP PIN, taxpayers could easily lose an IRS-issued credential because it would be used only when filing a tax return.

- **Implementing a risk-based authentication strategy that would select returns for additional authentication checks if the returns are high risk.** For example, IRS could match return information (e.g., name, address, SSN) against third-party databases to assess the risk that the identity has been stolen before IRS accepts the return for processing. High-risk returns would require the filer to answer authentication questions to confirm their identity, whereas low-risk returns would be processed. According to one analytics company we interviewed, because this option could be an automated, computerized match that would not require any action from taxpayers, it would limit burden on low-risk taxpayers because they would not be subject to additional authentication checks. Although the analytics company official stated that this authentication option has been used by some states, he also acknowledged that there are no data available about its effectiveness in combating IDT refund fraud at the state level.

IRS Is Creating an Authentication Group to Examine Options, but Lacks a Plan for Identifying and Assessing Tools

According to IRS officials, the agency is in the initial stages of creating an authentication group aimed at centralizing several prior ad hoc efforts to authenticate taxpayers across IRS services (e.g., online, telephone calls, walk-in services). While the group was not specifically designed in response to IDT refund fraud, improving authentication across IRS would likely advance IRS's ability to combat such fraud. IRS officials anticipate the group will consider options for improving authentication and will make recommendations to senior IRS executives. As of October 2014, the group was operating as a task team, with staff detailed from other IRS units. In its draft planning documentation, the authentication group outlined several initial high-level goals. Generally, they include:

- Centralize protection of IRS and taxpayers through integrated identity management;
- Centralize decisions and a strategic approach for authentication;
- Provide an avenue for tax administration through identity management;
- Provide an operational foundation for authentication;
- Provide a consistent operational approach to implementing authentication processes, including updating relevant *Internal Revenue Manual* sections;

- Improve the security of IRS interactions and transactions with internal and external stakeholders; and
- Coordinate the testing of authentication techniques (e.g., in-person or remote authentication through the Post Office or other venues).

The group has also documented short- and long-term priorities, including implementation plans. In recent discussions, agency officials said they would coordinate analysis of costs, benefits and risks with several IRS offices. However, a commitment to cost, benefit and risk analysis is not documented in the group's short- and long-term priorities. The draft planning documentation that we were given by IRS makes no mention of where such analyses would be included in IRS's priorities.

Federal guidance directs agencies to assess the costs, benefits and risks of government systems. OMB provides guidance to agencies for conducting economic cost-benefit and cost-effectiveness assessments that promote efficient resource allocation through well-informed decision making.[39] Specifically, these assessments should consider different alternatives to meet program objectives along with a discussion of costs and benefits. Further, OMB and NIST provide guidance for agencies to review new and existing electronic transactions to ensure that authentication processes provide the appropriate level of assurance.[40] Agencies can determine the appropriate level of assurance by conducting an assessment, mapping identified risks to the applicable assurance level, and selecting technology based on e-authentication technical guidance, among other steps. While we recognize that developing quantitative cost, benefit and risk estimates can be challenging or may not always be possible, qualitative analysis can also be informative, as discussed by OMB guidance.

Without analysis of costs, benefits and risks, IRS and Congress will not have quantitative information that could inform decisions about whether and how much to invest in the various authentication options. These decisions could include which authentication options to pursue (e.g., expanding the IP PIN or issuing a credential), where in the tax filing process authentication would be required (e.g., at the time of filing or after a return is flagged by IDT filters), and what level of assurance would be required (as detailed in OMB and NIST guidance). 41 Cost, benefit and risk estimates for authentication would have the additional benefit of allowing comparisons with other options for combating IDT refund fraud, such as pre-refund W-2 matching. Both approaches could have significant costs for taxpayers and IRS, so more information about the tradeoffs would help inform IRS and congressional decision making.

CONCLUSION

IDT refund fraud is a large, continually evolving threat that is costing taxpayers billions of dollars per year. Honest taxpayers who have had fraudulent tax returns filed in their name have the burden of proving to IRS who they are and waiting for delayed refunds. IRS has poured resources into trying to clean up the tax accounts of the honest victims and is playing a losing game of "pay and chase" with the thieves. A strategy that avoids these costs would be one to prevent fraudulent refunds from being issued in the first place. While IRS has a variety of preventive measures in place, the *Taxonomy* estimates show that additional preventative efforts could have significant benefits.

IRS's *Taxonomy* estimates are one part of improving IRS's prevention strategies. Because the *Taxonomy* helps IRS understand how and to what extent IDT refund fraud is evading IRS defenses, it can focus attention on where the risk is greatest and can help improve the design of IRS's IDT filters. To reap the most benefit from the *Taxonomy*, decision makers—both IRS managers and Congress—need to understand how reliable the estimates are. Given the difficulties in estimating refund fraud, reporting only point estimates risks misleading decision makers about the extent and nature of IDT refund fraud. While a point estimate might lead to one decision, a range that reflects the uncertainty may lead decision makers to a different decision.

We previously recommended that IRS develop cost-benefit information on pre-refund W-2 matching, which IRS has committed to implementing. Another tool that IRS is beginning to implement is device identification, which has potential benefits at low costs. IRS has limited information about the costs, benefits and risks of a third option, taxpayer authentication. The lack of this information could hinder decision makers' ability to select which option (or combination of options) is most cost beneficial.

RECOMMENDATIONS

To improve the reliability of *Taxonomy* estimates for future filing seasons, the Commissioner of Internal Revenue should follow relevant best practices outlined in the *GAO Cost Guide* by taking the following two actions:

- Documenting the underlying analysis justifying cost-influencing assumptions, and
- Reporting the inherent imprecision and uncertainty of the estimates. For example, IRS could provide a range of values for its *Taxonomy* estimates.

To ensure relevant information is available to decision makers, we recommend that the Commissioner of Internal Revenue estimate and document the costs, benefits and risks of possible options for taxpayer authentication, in accordance with OMB and NIST guidance.

AGENCY COMMENTS AND OUR EVALUATION

We provided a draft of this product to the Commissioner of Internal Revenue for review and comment. IRS agreed with our recommendations. With regard to our first recommendation, IRS stated that it will follow best practices in the *GAO Cost Guide* for documenting the rationale supporting assumptions used in the *Taxonomy* estimates. IRS also stated that it will supplement its revenue lost estimates by reporting the inherent imprecision and uncertainty of estimates, subject to the availability of data and resources.

While we acknowledged IRS's resource limitations in the report, we also stated that reporting a point estimate without a range or some other indication of uncertainty could provide a false sense of precision about refunds prevented and paid. This false sense of precision could affect decisions about how to allocate resources to combat IDT refund fraud. Given the importance of these estimates, providing the proper context is also important. With regard to our second recommendation, IRS stated that its authentication group will develop a repeatable process to estimate and document the costs, benefits and risks of possible options for taxpayer authentication, in accordance with OMB and NIST guidance. However, the scope and analysis may be limited due to available resources and time. IRS also provided technical comments on figure

1, which we revised to acknowledge that the examples provided are for IDT refund fraud cases detected after refund issuance.

James R. White
Director, Tax Issues Strategic Issues

APPENDIX I: OBJECTIVES, SCOPE, AND METHODOLOGY

This report assesses (1) the quality of the Internal Revenue Service (IRS) *Identity Theft Taxonomy's (Taxonomy)* estimates of the cost of identity theft (IDT) refund fraud, and (2) IRS's progress in developing processes to track device identification numbers and to enhance taxpayer authentication.[1] The report discusses IDT refund fraud and not employment fraud.

To assess the quality of the *Taxonomy's* estimates of IDT refund fraud, we reviewed the *Taxonomy's* methodology and estimates for filing season 2013 and evaluated them against selected best practices in the *GAO Cost Estimating and Assessment Guide (GAO Cost Guide)* that were applicable to the *Taxonomy* and consistent with IRS and Office of Management and Budget (OMB) information quality guidelines (see text box).[2]

In addition, these best practices are relevant because the *Taxonomy* is an estimate of the amount of revenue lost to IDT refund fraud—a cost to taxpayers. To develop this guide, our cost experts assessed the measures consistently applied by cost-estimating organizations throughout the federal government and industry; based upon this assessment, cost experts then considered best practices for the development of reliable cost estimates.

During our assessment of the *Taxonomy*, we interviewed IRS officials to better understand IRS's methodology. We also discussed the *GAO Cost Guide's* best practices with IRS officials who generally agreed with their applicability to the *Taxonomy*. IRS officials said many of the best practices are relevant to the *Taxonomy*, but questioned the applicability of best practices related to sensitivity and uncertainty analyses. They also questioned whether the *Taxonomy* itself was a cost estimate. We consulted with our cost estimating experts and concluded that the *Taxonomy* is a cost estimate because it is IRS's estimate of the amount of revenue lost due to IDT refund fraud. Further, given the importance of the *Taxonomy* and the fact that changes in the assumptions IRS makes and includes in the estimates substantially affect results, we believe providing information about the uncertainty of the *Taxonomy* estimates is warranted (as discussed in more detail in the report).

Selected Best Practices in Cost Estimating

Objective, reliable cost estimates

- Include all relevant costs.
- Document all cost-influencing ground rules and assumptions.
- Capture the source data used.
- Describe in sufficient detail the calculations performed and the estimating methodology used to derive each element's cost.
- Describe step by step how the estimate was developed so that a cost analyst
- unfamiliar with the program can understand what was done and replicate it.
- Provide evidence that the cost estimate was reviewed and accepted by management.
- Are regularly updated to reflect significant changes in the methodology.
- Contain few mistakes.
- Include a sensitivity analysis.
- Include a risk and uncertainty analysis.
- Are not overly conservative or optimistic, but are based on an assessment of most likely costs.

Source: GAO Cost Estimating and Assessment Guide, GAO-09-3SP. | GAO-15-119

To analyze IRS's *Taxonomy* against the best practices, we reviewed *Taxonomy* documentation, conducted manual data testing for obvious errors, compared underlying data to IRS's *Refund Fraud & Identity Theft Global Report*, and conducted numerous interviews with IRS officials to understand the methodology the IRS used to create estimates. We also confirmed *Taxonomy* components where we had data available to cross check. We developed an overall assessment rating for each best practice using the following definitions:

- **Not met.** IRS provided no evidence that satisfies any portion of the best practice.
- **Minimally met.** IRS provided evidence that satisfies a small portion of the best practice.
- **Partially met.** IRS provided evidence that satisfies about half of the best practice.

- **Substantially met.** IRS provided evidence that satisfies a large portion of the best practice.
- **Met.** IRS provided complete evidence that satisfies the entire best practice.

To assess IRS's progress in developing processes to track device identification numbers and to enhance taxpayer authentication, we reviewed *Internal Revenue Manual* sections detailing IRS's Identity Protection Program and IRS documentation for several tools developed to combat IDT refund fraud. We also interviewed IRS officials to learn about these efforts. These included the Identity Protection Personal Identification Number, device identification, authentication group, and other efforts related to identity authentication. We compared IRS's authentication group's planning document to OMB's guidance on cost-benefit analyses, as well as OMB and the National Institute for Standards and Technology (NIST) guidance on assessing levels of assurance for taxpayer authentication.[3] We interviewed NIST officials to better understand the methodology used in their cost-benefit analysis of a credential-based taxpayer authentication system and to gather input on the advantages and disadvantages of this type of system.

To learn about additional actions IRS could take to prevent IDT refund fraud, we interviewed associations representing software companies, return preparers, and financial institutions. To help ensure our analysis covered a variety of viewpoints, we selected a nonprobability sample of 18 associations and stakeholders with differing positions and characteristics, based on IRS documentation and suggestions, our prior work, and other information. For example, to select associations representing financial institutions, we considered (among other factors) the size and type of institutions they represented (e.g., large or small banks, credit unions, and prepaid debit card companies). Because we used a nonprobability sample, the views of these associations are not generalizable to all potential third parties.

When possible, we used a standard set of questions in interviewing these associations and summarized the results of the semistructured interviews. However, as needed, we also sought perspectives on additional questions tailored to these associations' expertise and sought their opinions on key issues. To determine the feasibility of various options and the challenges of pursuing them, we then communicated with IRS offices including (1) Privacy, Government Liaison, and Disclosure; (2) Customer Accounts Services, and (3) Return Integrity and Correspondence Services.

We conducted this performance audit from August 2013 to January 2015 in accordance with generally accepted government auditing standards.

Those standards require that we plan and perform the audit to obtain sufficient, appropriate evidence to provide a reasonable basis for our findings and conclusions based on our audit objectives. We believe that the evidence obtained provides a reasonable basis for our findings and conclusions based on our audit objectives.

Table 3. List of Third Parties Interviewed

Software and Analytics Companies	1. Equifax 2. H&R Blocka 3. Intuit 4. LexisNexis 5. SAS
Tax Software and Return Preparer Associations and Advisory Committees	6. American Coalition for Taxpayer Rights 7. American Institute of CPAs 8. Electronic Tax Administration Advisory Committee 9. Free File Alliance
Financial Institution and Payment Associations	10. American Bankers Association 11. BITSb 12. The Clearing House 13. Credit Union National Associationc 14. NACHA – The Electronic Payments Association 15. National Association of Federal Credit Unions 16. Network Branded Prepaid Card Association
Others	17. Federation of Tax Administrators 18. National Taxpayer Advocate

Source: GAO. | GAO-15-119.

[a] Also offers in-person tax preparation and banking services.

[b] Technology policy division of the Financial Services Roundtable. BITS is not an acronym. At one time, BITS stood for "Banking Industry Technology Secretariat." However, with financial modernization and the emergence of integrated financial services companies, that term is no longer used.

[c] Provided written comments.

APPENDIX II: SUMMARY OF TOOLS TO COMBAT IDENTITY THEFT REFUND FRAUD

The Internal Revenue Service (IRS) has developed multiple tools to combat identity theft (IDT) refund fraud. IDT detection occurs at three stages of the refund process: (1) before the IRS accepts tax returns, (2) during IRS's tax return processing, and (3) after IRS issues tax refunds to taxpayers (or fraudsters). IRS uses some of these tools currently, while others are under development or were recommended by one of our prior reports.[1] Table 4 describes each tool and its status.

Table 4. Overview of Current and Potential IRS Tools Used to Combat Identity Theft Refund Fraud, by Processing Stage

Processing Stage	Tool	Description	Status
Pre-acceptance	Identity Protection Personal Identification Number (IP PIN)	IRS provides single-use identification numbers to IDT victims who have confirmed their identities. IRS offered a limited IP PIN pilot in 2014. For details, see GAO-14-633 and GAO-13-132T.	Current program
	Automatic electronic filing (e-file) checks	IRS authenticates taxpayers during e-filing using self-select personal identification numbers (PINs), the prior year's adjusted gross income (AGI), and e-file PINs.	Current program
		Self-select PINs require taxpayers to provide their prior year's self-created PIN. *E-file PINs* require taxpayers to authenticate certain information, such as the taxpayer's name, Social Security number (SSN), date of birth, address, and filing status.	

Processing Stage	Tool	*Description*	Status
	Duplicate return reject	IRS automatically rejects returns that are e-filed using a given Taxpayer Identification Number (such as an SSN) when that SSN has been filed on a previously filed return. This prevents multiple fraudulent returns being filed with the same Taxpayer Identification Number. While IRS officials are aware of e-file rejects (including duplicate return rejects), they do not know if the rejects are due to IDT refund fraud or other reasons.	Current program
	Duplicate return reject for married filing jointly returns	IRS currently uses a manual process to detect fraudulent married filing jointly returns in cases where the same Taxpayer Identification Number (such as a SSN) has been listed on multiple returns with more than two different spousal SSNs. IRS is identifying ways to automate this process during the pre-acceptance stage, according to IRS officials.	Program in development
	Identity credential	Credentials—consisting of passwords or tokens— enable taxpayers to actively confirm their identities through authentication questions. Credentials could be received from IRS or a third party, and could be used when filing taxes and conducting other transactions.	Potential authentication option

Table 4. (Continued)

Processing Stage	Tool	Description	Status
During Return Processing	Pre-refund Form W-2, *Wage and Tax Statement*(W-2) matching	IRS validates taxpayer-reported return information (e.g., wages and compensation) with employer-reported information by matching W-2 information to tax returns before issuing refunds.a	Program under consideration/ related GAO recommendationb
	Identity theft and other fraud filters	Automated filters screen returns for characteristics of IDT (or other) fraud, or screen for clusters of returns with similar characteristics. For details, see GAO-14-633 and GAO-13-132T.	Current program
	Return Review Program (RRP)	An automated system that is intended to detect criminal and civil noncompliance through sophisticated models and analysis.	Program in developmentc
	Authentication questionsd	IRS confirms the identities of taxpayers whose returns are selected by its identity theft and other fraud filters, or who participate in the IP PIN pilot.	Current program
		Authentication questions ask about personal information that only the taxpayer should know (e.g., Who is your mortgage lender? Which of the following is your previous address?)	

Processing Stage	Tool	Description	Status
	Identity theft indicators	IRS places markers on taxpayer accounts that denote IDT problems. Indicators speed resolution by making a taxpayer's IDT problems visible to all IRS personnel with account access. For details, see GAO-14-633 and GAO-13-132T.	Current program
	Manual pattern matching	During tax return processing, IRS analysts look for patterns of suspicious activity to determine if a return is fraudulent and requires screening.	Current program
	Device identification analysis	Analyzes the unique identification number associated with a device (e.g., computer, tablet) to identify fraudulent returns filed from the same device.	Program in development
	Risk-based authentication strategy	Taxpayer returns are screened against third-party databases to assess the risk that the identity has been stolen before IRS accepts the return for processing. High-risk returns would require the taxpayer to answer authentication questions to confirm his or her identity, whereas low-risk returns would be processed.	Potential authentication option
Post-refund	Third-party leads	*External Leads Program*-third parties (e.g., financial institutions or software companies) report suspected IDT refund fraud.	Current programe

Table 4. (Continued)

Processing Stage	Tool	Description	Status
		Opt-In Program – financial institutions electronically reject suspicious refunds. For details on both programs, see GAO-14-633.	
	Taxpayer alerts	A taxpayer notifies IRS of IDT (e.g., calls IRS because of a duplicate return reject, or responds to an IRS compliance notice). For details, see GAO-14-633.	Current program
	Information return matching	IRS finds IDT refund fraud when it matches tax return data to information returns as part of the Automated Underreporter (AUR) program, which matches tax return data to information returns, such as Form W-2, *Wage and Tax Statement*(W-2). The legitimate taxpayer may not be aware of a stolen identity until after receiving a notice indicating the income and/or payment information IRS has on file is missing or does not match the information reported on the tax return.	Current program

Source: GAO analysis of IRS information. | GAO-15-119.

Note: This table provides examples of IRS tools, but it is not an exhaustive list. Tools listed focus on IDT prevention and detection, but not IDT customer service or enforcement efforts.

[a]Currently, IRS cannot do such matching because employers' wage data are unavailable until months after IRS issues most refunds. To facilitate the use of W-2 information to help combat IDT refund fraud, the Department of the Treasury

(Treasury) proposed to Congress that the W-2 deadlines be moved to January 31. We found that IRS had not fully assessed the impacts of this proposal. Treasury also requested authority to reduce the 250-return threshold for electronically filing information returns. Without this change, some employers' paper W-2s could not be available for IRS matching until much later in the year, due to the additional time needed to process paper forms. For details, see GAO-14-633.

[b]GAO recommended that IRS assess the benefits and costs of accelerating W-2 deadlines and provide information to Congress on (1) IRS systems and work processes that would need to be adjusted, (2) potential impacts on taxpayers, IRS, the Social Security Administration, and third parties; and (3) any other changes that may be needed. In November 2014, IRS reported that it had convened an internal working group to address our recommendations and that it anticipated implementing our recommendations by July 2015. In addition, GAO suggested that Congress should consider providing the Secretary of the Treasury with the regulatory authority to lower the threshold for electronic filing of W-2s from 250 returns annually to between 5 and 10 returns, as appropriate. For details, see GAO-14-633.

[c]IRS officials told us that the next version of RRP is on a "strategic pause" while IRS officials clarify functionality amidst budget constraints. However, IRS piloted one component to detect IDT refund fraud for some filing season 2014 returns, and it plans to use this system in filing season 2015.

[d]Authentication questions are also known as "knowledge-based authentication questions" or "out of wallet" questions.

[e]Related to this, GAO recommended that IRS (1) provide aggregated information on the success of external party leads in identifying suspicious returns and emerging trends to relevant lead-generating third parties, and (2) develop a set of metrics to track external leads by the submitting third party. In November 2014, IRS reported that it is developing a reporting methodology and metrics to address our recommendations. For more information, see GAO-14-633.

APPENDIX III: HOW ASSUMPTIONS AFFECT *IDENTITY THEFT TAXONOMY (TAXONOMY)* RESULTS – TWO EXAMPLES

The Internal Revenue Service (IRS) developed the *Taxonomy* for a number of reasons, including the need to monitor both the volume and cost of identity theft (IDT) refund fraud attempts and the effectiveness of IDT defenses over time. *Taxonomy* estimates are based on IRS's administrative records of known IDT refund fraud (e.g., data on the number of duplicate returns). The *Taxonomy* also estimates IDT refunds by, for example, identifying returns with the characteristics of IDT refund fraud, as detected by the Automated Underreporter (AUR) program.[1]

Best practices within the *GAO Cost Estimating and Assessment Guide* suggest that sensitivity and uncertainty analyses should be used to determine whether assumptions are potentially introducing error into an estimate.[2] The following examples demonstrate how the assumptions IRS makes (and includes in its estimates of IDT refund fraud) substantially affect *Taxonomy* results.

Example 1: IRS's Analysis Demonstrates that Assumptions Substantially Affect *Taxonomy* Estimates

As shown in figure 4, $3.0 billion of the estimated $5.8 billion in IDT refunds paid in filing season 2013 are based on estimates developed using AUR data from information return matching (we refer to this part of the *Taxonomy* as the "AUR category"). To estimate the AUR category, IRS uses assumptions based on the characteristics of past IDT refund fraud. These characteristics enable IRS to identify which information return mismatches are IDT returns. IRS officials must develop assumptions about the IDT refund fraud characteristics because without conducting a tax return audit, it is impossible for officials to determine whether mismatches are IDT or are some other type of noncompliant return (i.e., a legitimate taxpayer makes a mistake or purposely files a noncompliant return). As IRS develops its assumptions, it uses them to help estimate which information return mismatches are noncompliant returns (the turquoise dots in figure 4) and which are IDT returns (the purple dots).

As further illustrated in figure 4, IRS chose assumptions that it believed best balanced comprehensiveness (that most IDT returns are likely included but legitimate returns are also included) with certainty (that many of the returns selected were IDT and include few, if any, legitimate returns). A completely comprehensive estimate (as illustrated by the larger circle) would be an overcount and could result in an IDT refund estimate about 26 times greater than IRS's current estimate, according to our analysis of the *Taxonomy*. In contrast, a completely certain estimate (as illustrated in the smaller circle) would be an undercount and would result in an IDT refund estimate that is 25 times less than IRS's current estimate.

Using these two extremes would likely result in an "IDT refunds paid" estimate range that is too broad. Since IRS has not conducted an uncertainty analysis, we do not know the range that likely encompasses most cases of IDT.

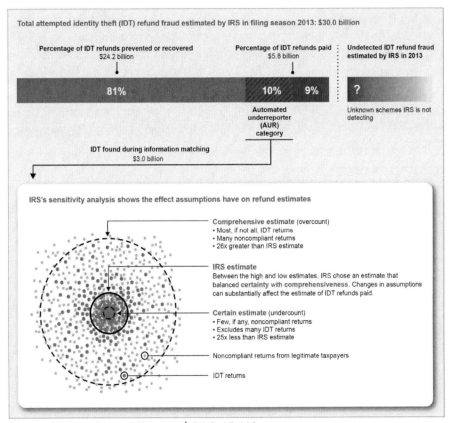

Source: GAO analysis of IRS data. | GAO-15-119.

Note: The figure above is shown for illustrative purposes; the actual distribution of IDT versus noncompliant returns from legitimate taxpayers is unknown. To develop the magnitude measures above, we divided IRS's highest and lowest AUR category estimate by the estimate IRS chose in filing season 2013. Using these two extremes would likely result in too broad of a range in IDT refunds paid estimates.

Figure 4. How Assumptions Affect *Taxonomy* Estimates Based on Data from Information Return Matching.

Example 2: The *Taxonomy* Does Not Account for Variability in Refund Values

IRS uses an average refund value in certain *Taxonomy* categories, instead of using the actual value of each individual refund counted in the estimate. Therefore, it is likely that the total estimates of "IDT refunds paid" and "IDT refunds prevented" are imprecise. For example, figure 5 demonstrates how IRS developed its estimate of the value of refunds prevented by rejecting electronically filed returns (e-file reject).[3] To develop its $6.2 billion estimate, IRS multiplied the number of e-file rejects (1.06 million) by the average refund associated with IDT returns caught by IRS IDT filters and other fraud defenses ($5,804).

Table 5. Potential Estimates of E-file Rejects Using Different IRS IDT Defenses, Calendar Year 2013

IDT defense	Average refund (in dollars per return)	Number of e-file rejects (in millions)	Total value ofrefunds preventedby e-file rejects (in billions)
Unpostable returnsa	$4,578	1.06	$4.9
Identity theft filters (Dependent Database)	$4,600	1.06	$4.9
Returns detected as part of a repeat "Operation Mass Mail" schemeb	$5,636	1.06	$6.0
Fraud filters (Electronic Fraud Detection System)	$7,422	1.06	$7.9
Returns detected as part of a new "Operation Mass Mail" schemeb	$8,235	1.06	$8.7
IRS estimate using average refund value for all IDT defenses	$5,804	1.06	$6.2

Source: GAO analysis of IRS *Refund Fraud and Identity Theft Global Report*, December 2013. | GAO-15-119.

[a]Returns are "unpostable" when they fail to pass validity checks within IRS systems. An account with certain identity theft indicators will cause a return to unpost.

[b]IRS defenses search for returns associated with the "Operation Mass Mail" scheme, where identity thieves use the stolen identities of Puerto Rican citizens and individuals from other U.S. territories.

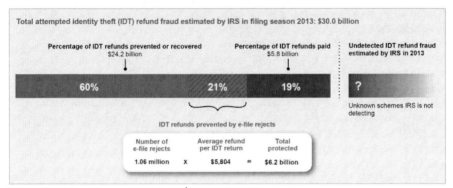

Source: GAO analysis of IRS data. | GAO-15-119.

Figure 5. Estimating Refunds Prevented Using E-file Rejects and Average Refunds, Filing Season 2013.

However, the average refund value of e-file returns detected by IRS IDT defenses can vary—indicating uncertainty in this estimate. For example, if IRS used the different average refunds in table 5 to develop its e-file reject estimate, the total could range from $4.9 billion to $8.7 billion.

End Notes

[1] This report discusses IDT refund fraud and not employment fraud. IDT employment fraud occurs when an identity thief uses a taxpayer's name and Social Security number to obtain a job.

[2] For more information, see GAO, *Identity Theft: Additional Actions Could Help IRS Combat the Large, Evolving Threat of Refund Fraud*, GAO-14-633 (Washington, D.C.: Aug. 20, 2014).

[3] A point estimate is a population estimate that is presented as a single statistic.

[4] GAO-14-633.

[5] Device identification is the unique number associated with an individual device, such as a laptop computer, used to electronically file a return.

[6] The *Taxonomy* estimates the number and cost of identified IDT refund fraud cases where (1) IRS prevented or recovered the fraudulent refunds, and (2) paid the fraudulent refunds.

[7] GAO, *GAO Cost Estimating and Assessment Guide: Best Practices for Developing and Managing Capital Program Costs*, GAO-09-3SP (Washington, D.C.: March 2009) and OMB, *Guidelines for Ensuring and Maximizing the Quality, Objectivity, Utility, and Integrity of Information Disseminated by Federal Agencies*, (Washington, D.C.: October 2001), accessed September 25, 2014, http://www.whitehouse.gov/omb/fedreg_final_ information_quality_guidelines.

[8] For details, see appendix I.

[9] OMB, *E-Authentication Guidance for Federal Agencies*, M-04-04 (Washington, D.C.: Dec. 16, 2003); *Circular A-94: Guidelines and Discount Rates for Benefit Cost Analysis of Federal*

Programs (Washington, D.C.: 1992); and NIST, *Electronic Authentication Guideline*, Special Publication 800-63-2, (August 2013).

[10] IRS's "Where's My Refund" website had about 201 million inquiries in fiscal year 2013, according to IRS data. For 2014, IRS announced that it would generally issue refunds in less than 21 days after receiving a tax return.

[11] IRS, *Strategic Plan: FY2014-2017*, (Washington, D.C.: June 2014).

[12] Since 2010, the agency has absorbed approximately $900 million in budget cuts while also facing an increasing workload due to legislative mandates, priority programs—such as the implementation and administration of various tax provisions enacted in the Patient Protection and Affordable Care Act—and IDT refund fraud.

[13] See GAO-14-633 for more details on IRS's IP PIN program.

[14] GAO, *Tax Refunds: IRS is Exploring Verification Improvements, but Needs to Better Manage Risks*, GAO-13-515 (Washington, D.C.: June 4, 2013).

[15] DDb incorporates IRS, Department of Health & Human Services, and Social Security Administration data to identify compliance issues involving IDT, refundable credits, and prisoners. EFDS is a system built in the mid-1990s to detect taxpayer fraud.

[16] IRS has paused further RRP development due to budget constraints and a need to ensure alignment of RRP goals with IRS's strategic vision for IDT and refund fraud detection, among other reasons, according to IRS officials.

[17] The *Global Report* tracks information about identity theft incidents and IRS detection and resolution efforts using multiple sources within IRS.

[18] IRS officials must develop these assumptions because without conducting a tax return audit, it is impossible for officials to determine whether mismatches are IDT returns or other noncompliant returns (i.e., a legitimate taxpayer makes a mistake or purposely files a noncompliant return).

[19] This figure is an update to a similar figure that appeared in GAO-14-633. Since we issued GAO-14-633, IRS's estimate of IDT refunds paid increased from $5.2 billion to $5.8 billion, as will be discussed later.

[20] Administration of Barack Obama, *Executive Order 13681, Improving the Security of Consumer Financial Transactions* (Washington, D.C.: Oct. 17, 2014).

[21] IRS developed these guidelines pursuant to the Treasury and General Government Appropriations Act for Fiscal Year 2001 (P.L. 106-554, § 515).

[22] OMB, *Guidelines for Ensuring and Maximizing the Quality, Objectivity, Utility, and Integrity of Information Disseminated by Federal Agencies*, (Washington, D.C.: October 2001), accessed September 25, 2014, http://www.whitehouse.gov/omb/fedreg_final_information_quality_guidelines.

[23] GAO-09-3SP.

[24] There may be some types of error that our data reliability testing was unable to detect. For example, we cross-checked *Taxonomy* estimates against the *Global Report*; however, if the *Global Report* itself contains errors, our data reliability testing would not detect these errors.

[25] The AUR program matches information returns to tax returns and pursues discrepancies.

[26] A sensitivity analysis (also known as "what if" analysis) examines the effect changing assumptions has on the estimate by changing one assumption at a time. It involves recalculating the estimate using differing assumptions to develop ranges of potential estimates.

[27] Risk and uncertainty analysis recognizes the potential for error and captures the cumulative effect that assumptions have on the cost estimate. It involves using methods to develop a range of costs around a point estimate.

[28] For some IDT metrics used to develop *Taxonomy* estimates in categories 1-3, the *Global Report* provides detail on the volume of IDT returns but has no detail on the refunds associated with those returns. For example, the *Global Report* provides data on the number of e-filed returns rejected due to a missing or incorrect IP PIN, but does not have data on the refunds associated with those returns. In other cases, IRS defenses do not distinguish IDT from other types of fraud. For example, the Electronic Fraud Detection System (EFDS) detects fraudulent returns, but in some cases does not differentiate between whether the returns are IDT or noncompliant. Therefore, to develop its *Taxonomy* category 2 estimates, IRS develops assumptions on the percent of returns detected by EFDS that are IDT refund fraud.

[29] GAO, *Improper Payments: Remaining Challenges and Strategies for Governmentwide Reduction Efforts*, GAO-12-573T (Washington, D.C.: Mar. 28, 2012).

[30] IRS, *Publication 1345, Handbook for Authorized IRS e-File Provider of Individual Income Tax Returns* (Washington, D.C.: Nov. 17, 2014). Authorized e-file providers are tax professionals who are accepted into the electronic filing program and who transmit tax return information to the IRS.

[31] IRS already requires all tax software companies to identify the particular software package used to prepare tax returns using a three-letter source code on all electronically prepared paper returns. This was a change IRS implemented as a result of our prior recommendation. See GAO, *Many Taxpayers Rely on Tax Software and IRS Needs to Assess Associated Risks*, GAO-09-297 (Washington, D.C.: Feb. 25, 2009).

[32] We asked an open-ended question about how IRS could combat IDT. Three of the six companies and associations offered this specific information. The others were silent on the e-file PIN.

[33] Authentication questions can draw on information in public records databases (e.g., credit records) or from the individual's tax records.

[34] For returns flagged by fraud filters, IRS sends a letter asking the taxpayer to confirm his or her identity by calling IRS, by providing a written response, or by answering online authentication questions.

[35] IRS found that 5 percent of the "high risk" group (likely identity thieves) correctly answered the authentication questions. In contrast, 19 percent of the "low risk" group (likely legitimate taxpayers) that attempted to authenticate did not correctly answer the questions. To develop this analysis, IRS categorized returns into "high risk" and "low risk" groups using characteristics such as whether tax return data matched information return data submitted by third parties.

[36] We asked an open-ended question about how IRS could combat IDT. Three of the companies and associations offered this specific information and one company recommended an alternative option. The others were silent on expanding the IP PIN.

[37] A third-party issued credential would be aligned with standards established by the National Strategy for Trusted Identities in Cyberspace (NSTIC), a White House initiative to develop an online environment where organizations follow agreed upon standards to obtain and authenticate their digital identities.

[38] NIST, *Planning Report 13-2, Economic Case Study: The Impact of NSTIC on the Internal Revenue Service* (July 2013).

[39] OMB Circular A-94.

[40] OMB M-04-04 and NIST Special Publication 800-63-2. OMB and NIST guidance defines four levels of assurance. Each assurance level describes the agency's degree of certainty in terms of consequences of authentication errors and misuse of credentials. For example, level 3 provides high confidence in the asserted identity's validity and would require two-factor authentication (e.g., a username and password plus a token displaying a new PIN every minute).

[41] OMB M-04-04 and NIST 800-63-2.

End Notes for Appendix I

[1] Device identification is the unique number associated with an individual device, such as a laptop computer, used to electronically file a return.

[2] GAO, *GAO Cost Estimating and Assessment Guide: Best Practices for Developing and Managing Capital Program Costs*, GAO-09-3SP (Washington, D.C.: March 2009) and OMB, *Guidelines for Ensuring and Maximizing the Quality, Objectivity, Utility, and Integrity of Information Disseminated by Federal Agencies*, (Washington, D.C.: October 2001), accessed September 25, 2014, http://www.whitehouse.gov/omb/fedreg_final_information_quality_guidelines. IRS developed information quality guidelines to ensure that information the agency reports is objective. Objectivity, as defined in OMB quality guidelines, involves ensuring information is reliable, accurate, and unbiased. Objectivity also involves presenting information in a clear, complete, and unbiased manner.

[3] OMB, *E-Authentication Guidance for Federal Agencies*, M-04-04 (Washington, D.C.: Dec. 16, 2003); *Circular A-94: Guidelines and Discount Rates for Benefit Cost Analysis of Federal Programs* (Washington, D.C.: 1992); and NIST, *Electronic Authentication Guideline*, Special Publication 800-63-2, (August 2013).

End Note for Appendix II

[1] GAO, *Identity Theft: Additional Actions Could Help IRS Combat the Large, Evolving Threat of Refund Fraud*, GAO-14-633 (Washington, D.C.: Aug. 20, 2014).

End Notes for Appendix III

[1] The AUR program matches information returns (such as Form W-2, *Wage and Tax Statement*) to tax returns and pursues discrepancies after the filing season.

[2] A sensitivity analysis (also known as "what if" analysis) examines the effect changing assumptions has on the estimate by changing one assumption at a time. It involves recalculating the estimate using differing assumptions to develop ranges of potential estimates. Risk and uncertainty analysis recognizes the potential for error and captures the cumulative effect that assumptions have on the cost estimate. It involves using methods to develop a range of costs around a point estimate. See *GAO Cost Estimating and Assessment*

Guide: Best Practices for Developing and Managing Capital Program Costs, GAO-09-3SP, (Washington, D.C.: March 2009).

[3] E-file rejects can occur, for example, when a return is electronically filed without an Identity Protection Personal Identification Number.

In: Identity Theft Tax Refund Fraud   ISBN: 978-1-63482-602-0
Editor: Lucas Haynes   © 2015 Nova Science Publishers, Inc.

Chapter 3

PRISONER TAX REFUND FRAUD: DELAYS CONTINUE IN COMPLETING AGREEMENTS TO SHARE INFORMATION WITH PRISONS, AND REPORTS TO CONGRESS ARE NOT TIMELY OR COMPLETE[*]

Treasury Inspector General for Tax Administration

HIGHLIGHTS

Highlights of Reference Number: 2014-40-091 to the Internal Revenue Service Commissioner for the Wage and Investment Division.

Impact on Taxpayers

Refund fraud associated with prisoner Social Security Numbers remains a significant problem for tax administration. The number of fraudulent tax returns filed using a prisoner's Social Security Number that were identified by the IRS

---

[*] This is an edited, reformatted and augmented version of a report, Reference Number: 2014-40-091, issued September 25, 2014.
Note: Some text in the original document has been replaced (redacted) with the following notation: **2**.

increased from more than 37,000 tax returns in Calendar Year 2007 to more than 137,000 tax returns in Calendar Year 2012. The refunds claimed on these tax returns increased from $166 million to $1 billion.

Why TIGTA Did the Audit

This audit was initiated because prior TIGTA reports identified concerns with the IRS's efforts to identify and prevent prisoner tax fraud. The overall objective was to evaluate the effectiveness of the IRS's corrective actions to identify and reduce prisoner fraud.

What TIGTA Found

TIGTA found that the IRS has not yet shared fraudulent prisoner tax return information with Federal or State prison officials. TIGTA also found that the required annual prisoner fraud reports to Congress are not timely and that the reports do not address the extent to which prisoners may be filing fraudulent tax returns using a different individual's SSN. TIGTA also followed up on a condition identified in a past review and found that IRS processes still do not ensure that all tax returns filed using a prisoner Social Security Number are assigned a prisoner indicator.

What TIGTA Recommended

TIGTA recommended that the Commissioner, Wage and Investment Division, ensure that Memorandums of Understanding are timely established with the Federal Bureau of Prisons and all State Departments of Corrections. The IRS should also ensure that the required annual report on prisoner fraud is issued to Congress timely and that processes are developed to identify tax returns filed that have the same characteristics of confirmed fraudulent prisoner tax returns and determine whether these tax returns should be included in the annual report to Congress. The IRS should also ensure that all tax returns that are filed using a prisoner Social Security Number are assigned a prisoner indicator.

The IRS agreed with four of the six recommendations. The IRS did not agree to develop a process to identify other tax returns that have the same characteristics as confirmed fraudulent prisoner returns. Without such processes the IRS annual report will not include, as required, information related to the filing of all false and fraudulent tax returns by prisoners.

In addition, the IRS did not agree to correct a computer programming error that resulted in its not assigning a prisoner indicator to 3,139 tax returns TIGTA identified. Without the proper assignment of a prisoner indicator, the tax returns are not sent through those fraud detection filters specific to a prisoner-filed tax return.

TREASURY INSPECTOR GENERAL
FOR TAX ADMINISTRATION

DEPARTMENT OF THE TREASURY
WASHINGTON, D.C. 20220

September 25, 2014

MEMORANDUM FOR COMMISSIONER, WAGE AND INVESTMENT DIVISION

FROM: Michael E. McKenney
                 Deputy Inspector General for Audit

SUBJECT: Final Audit Report – Prisoner Tax Refund Fraud: Delays Continue in
                 Completing Agreements to Share Information With Prisons, and
                 Reports to Congress Are Not Timely or Complete (Audit # 201340016)

This report presents the results of our review to evaluate the effectiveness of the Internal Revenue Service's (IRS) corrective actions to identify and reduce prisoner fraud. We conducted follow-up testing to evaluate the effectiveness of the IRS's actions to address recommendations made in a previous Treasury Inspector General for Tax Administration report. In addition, we evaluated the IRS's compliance with the continuing provisions of the Inmate Tax Fraud Prevention Act of 2008[1] and the American Taxpayer Relief Act of 2012.[2] This audit is included in our Fiscal Year 2014 Annual Audit Plan and addresses the major management challenge of Fraudulent Claims and Improper Payments.

Management's complete response to the draft report is included as Appendix V.

Copies of this report are also being sent to the IRS managers affected by the report recommendations. If you have questions, please contact me or Russell P. Martin, Acting Assistant Inspector General for Audit (Returns Processing and Account Services).

---

[1] Pub. L. No. 110-428, 122 Stat. 4839.
[2] Pub. L. No. 112-240, 126 Stat. 2313.

ABBREVIATIONS

EFDS   Electronic Fraud Detection System
IRS   Internal Revenue Service
MOU   Memorandum of Understanding
SSN   Social Security Number
TIGTA   Treasury Inspector General for Tax Administration

BACKGROUND

Tax refund fraud associated with prisoners remains a significant problem for tax administration. Figure 1 shows that the number of fraudulent tax returns filed using prisoner Social Security Numbers (SSN) that were identified by the Internal Revenue Service (IRS) increased from more than 37,000 tax returns in Calendar Year 2007 to more than 137,000 tax returns in Calendar Year 2012. The refunds claimed on these tax returns increased from $166 million to $1 billion.

**Figure 1. Fraudulent Tax Returns Filed Using
a Prisoner SSN for Calendar Years 2007 Through 2012**

Calendar Year	Fraudulent Tax Returns	Refunds Claimed (Millions)	Refunds Prevented (Millions)	Refunds Issued (Millions)
2007	37,447	$166	$137	$29
2008	47,898	$190	$162	$28
2009	44,944	$295	$256	$39
2010	91,434	$758	$722	$351
2011	186,483	$3,7252	$3,569	$156
2012	137,883	$1,005	$936	$70

Source: IRS Criminal Investigation and IRS Wage and Investment Division.

Legislation Enacted in an Effort to Address Fraud Perpetrated by Prisoners

- The Inmate Tax Fraud Prevention Act of 2008,3 signed October 15, 2008, gave the Secretary of the Treasury temporary authority to disclose to the head of the Federal Bureau of Prisons tax return information for individuals incarcerated in Federal prisons who the Secretary has determined may have filed or facilitated the filing of a fraudulent return. The act stated that no disclosure may be made after December 31, 2011.

- The act also requires the Secretary of the Treasury to provide an annual report to Congress on the filing of false or fraudulent tax returns by Federal and State prisoners. The first report completed by the IRS reporting on returns filed using a prisoner SSN was issued for Calendar Year 2009.

- *The Homebuyer Assistance and Improvement Act of 2010,*[4] enacted in July 2010, expanded the authority of the Secretary of the Treasury to also include disclosing prisoner tax return information to the State Departments of Corrections.[5] However, the expanded authority to disclose prisoner tax return information to the State Departments of Corrections as well as the Federal Bureau of Prisons still expired on December 31, 2011.

- *The United States–Korea Free Trade Agreement Implementation Act,*[6] signed October 21, 2011, requires the Federal Bureau of Prisons and State Departments of Corrections to provide the IRS with an electronic list of all the prisoners incarcerated within their prison system for any part of the prior two calendar years or the current calendar year through August 31. The Federal Bureau of Prisons and States were required to provide the first list of prisoners to the IRS not later than September 15, 2012, and are to provide updated information annually thereafter.

- *The American Taxpayer Relief Act of 2012,*[7] enacted in January 2013, expanded the Secretary of the Treasury's authority to share false prisoner tax return information with Federal and State prisons and gave the IRS permanent authority to share such information.

The authority for the IRS to disclose fraudulent prisoner tax return information with Federal and State Prisons became permanent in January 2013.

Prisoner File and the Electronic Fraud Detection System (EFDS)

To combat the continuing problem of refund fraud associated with tax returns filed using prisoner SSNs, the IRS compiles a list of prisoners (the Prisoner File) received from the Federal Bureau of Prisons and State Departments of Corrections. Various IRS offices and functions use the Prisoner File in an effort to prevent and detect fraud. The Prisoner File is the cornerstone of the IRS's efforts to prevent the issuance of fraudulent refunds to individuals filing false tax returns using a prisoner SSN. The EFDS is the primary system used by the IRS to identify tax returns filed using prisoner SSNs. The EFDS consists of a series of filters the IRS has designed to evaluate tax returns for potential fraud. Tax returns are processed through the EFDS, whereby the primary and secondary SSNs listed on the tax return are matched to the Prisoner File to determine if the tax return is filed using a prisoner SSN. If the SSN on the tax return matches a prisoner on the Prisoner File, a prisoner indicator is assigned to the tax return.

Tax returns assigned a prisoner indicator and that meet specific criteria are evaluated to determine if the tax return is fraudulent. This evaluation includes screening and verifying the wage and withholding information reported on the tax return. For example, in the screening process, a tax examiner reviews the tax return for income and withholding information, **2** *********************************2** *********** **********2**********. If the tax examiner concludes that the tax return is potentially fraudulent, the tax return is then sent for verification. In the verification process, a tax examiner attempts to contact the employer(s) associated with the reported income and withholding to confirm the income and withholding. If the tax examiner is unable to verify the income and withholding with the employer, the refund is frozen to prevent issuance.

Prior Treasury Inspector General for Tax Administration (TIGTA) reports identified concerns with IRS efforts to identify and prevent prisoner tax fraud

TIGTA has issued two reports on the IRS's efforts to combat prisoner fraud since Congress enacted the Inmate Tax Fraud Prevention Act of 2008. In December 2010[8] we reported that as of October 2010, the IRS had not completed required agreements to allow it to disclose prisoner tax return information to prison officials. As a result, no information had been disclosed to either the Federal Bureau of Prisons or State Departments of Corrections. In addition, we identified a lack of managerial oversight relating to the process used to compile the Prisoner File to ensure the accuracy and reliability of this file. In December 2012[9] we reported that despite increased efforts by the IRS to improve the accuracy of the Prisoner File, some prisoner information contained in the file is inaccurate. For example, the file contains incomplete records, and not all facilities that house prisoners reported prisoners. As such, controls used to ensure that the IRS identifies fraudulent refunds on tax returns prepared by prisoners are not fully effective. Further, the IRS's authority to disclose information to prisons expired on December 31, 2011,[10] which limited the ability of prison officials to curtail prisoners' continued abuse of the tax system. IRS management indicated that even though the authority to disclose information to prisons expired on December 31, 2011, the Federal Bureau of Prisons and State Departments of Corrections have been taking advantage of other voluntary IRS prisoner fraud programs that do not require a contract and have minimal cost to the Federal Bureau of Prisons and State Departments of Corrections. However, these programs only alert the Federal Bureau of Prisons, State Departments of Corrections, and the IRS to potential wrongdoing, whereas prisoner tax fraud data represent known fraud for which the Federal Bureau of Prisons and State Departments of Corrections can take action to address. Figure 2 details the recommendations and corrective actions contained in these reports.

**Figure 2. Prior TIGTA Audit Recommendations and
Actions Taken by the IRS to Address Recommendations**

TIGTA Report	Recommendation	Actions Taken to Date
2011-40-009 Dec. 2010	Work with the Department of the Treasury to seek legislation to extend the period of time the IRS has to disclose prisoner tax return information to the Federal Bureau of Prisons and State prison officials.	The American Taxpayer Relief Act of 2012 gave the IRS permanent authority to share false prisoner tax return information with Federal and State prisons.
	Provide Congress with a complete assessment of potential prisoner fraud by revising the annual report to include the total number of tax returns filed by prisoners, the number selected for fraud screening,	TheInmate Tax Fraud Prevention Act of 2008 requires the IRS to annually provide Congress a report that includes the number of false and fraudulent returns associated with prisoner filings.

Figure 2. (Continued)

TIGTA Report	Recommendation	Actions Taken to Date
	and the number verified false/fraudulent.	In addition, the IRS willrespond to future congressional requests pertaining to prison-related tax fraud.
	Ensure that all tax returns filed using a prisoner SSN are processed through the EFDS and receive a prisoner indicator.	Improvements were made to identify those individuals who are incarcerated, but no changes were made to the process to assign the prisoner indicator.
	Revise prisoner filters to verify the validity of the wages and withholding associated with prisoners incarcerated for a year who filed tax returns claiming a refund.	Filters are in place to verify the validity of wages and withholding associated with tax returns filed using a prisoner SSN. In addition, the IRS improved its processes for identifying individuals incarcerated for a full tax year.
	Develop a process to assess the reliability of data received from Federal and State prisons and communicate with prison facilities that provide missing or inaccurate information in an attempt to obtain corrected information.	The IRS identified structural or formatting errors and duplicated records in the 2012 Prisoner File. The IRS worked with the correctional systems to resolve the errors when possible.
2013-40-011 Dec. 2012	Ensure that the validation and verification of future IRS Prisoner Files include a check for a prisoner using a deceased individual's identity information and a comparison of the Institution and Prisoner Files to ensure that all facilities that house prisoners reported them.	The IRS implemented processes to identify prisoner SSNs with a Date of Death. If the prisoner information was verified with SocialSecurity Administration data, it was loaded into the EFDS with the "Validated" indicator left unchecked for the deceased prisoners on the prisoner file. Processes were also implemented in Calendar Year 2014 to ensure that prisons were reporting required prisoner information to the IRS.

TIGTA Report	Recommendation	Actions Taken to Date
	Legislation is needed that would permanently authorize the IRS to share data with the Federal and State prisons when it determines that prisoners may be using other individuals' identities.	The American Taxpayer Relief Act of 2012 improved and made permanent the authority for the IRS to disclose false prisoner tax return information to Federal and State prisons.

Source: TIGTA analysis of actions taken in response to prior audit reports.

This review is a follow-up of the IRS's efforts to address conditions identified in TIGTA's December 2010 report. Our review was performed with information obtained from the IRS Wage and Investment Division Headquarters Return Integrity and Correspondence Services function in Atlanta, Georgia, during the period July 2013 through June 2014. We conducted this performance audit in accordance with generally accepted government auditing standards. Those standards require that we plan and perform the audit to obtain sufficient, appropriate evidence to provide a reasonable basis for our findings and conclusions based on our audit objective. We believe that the evidence obtained provides a reasonable basis for our findings and conclusions based on our audit objective. Detailed information on our audit objective, scope, and methodology is presented in Appendix I. Major contributors to the report are listed in Appendix II.

RESULTS OF REVIEW

Fraudulent Prisoner Tax Return Information Has Yet to Be Shared with Federal or State Prison Officials

As of June 2014, the IRS has yet to complete needed agreements to begin sharing information related to false prisoner tax return information with Federal and State prison officials. This is despite the fact that the IRS was initially given the authority to share information with Federal prison officials in October 2008. Since October 2008, subsequent legislation temporarily expanded the IRS's authority to share information with State prison officials,[11] and permanent authority to share information was granted in January 2013. This authority was granted because Congress believes the ability of the IRS to share information with prison officials will enable them to take action to punish prisoners for perpetrating fraud and will help stop the abuse of our tax system.

According to the IRS, prior to the enactment of the American Taxpayer Relief Act of 2012, the IRS worked with the Department of the Treasury to create a legislative proposal to reauthorize disclosure and to address the most significant concerns related to the sharing of this information identified by Federal and State prison officials in Calendar Year 2011. Addressing these concerns was intended to ensure the success of prison administrative proceedings upon restarting the disclosure program. The proposed language that addressed these concerns was included in the American Taxpayer Relief Act of 2012.

IRS management also indicated that Memorandums of Understanding (MOU) establishing an information sharing agreement must be negotiated with the Federal Bureau of Prisons and each of the State Departments of Corrections. These MOUs outline how tax return information will be received, secured, and used by the receiving prison. In addition to the MOUs, the Federal Bureau of Prisons and the States must implement required information security safeguards before tax return information can be received.

The IRS Indicated That Previously Completed Mous Were No Longer Valid When Authority to Share Information Expired

The Inmate Tax Fraud Prevention Act of 2008 and the Homebuyer Assistance and Improvement Act of 2010 granted the IRS with the temporary authority to share false prisoner tax return information with the Federal Bureau of Prisons and State Departments of Corrections through December 2011. As of December 31, 2011, the IRS had finalized MOUs with the Federal Bureau of Prisons and 22 State Departments of Corrections under this temporary authority. However, IRS management indicated that the 23 MOUs the IRS had finalized were no longer valid once the temporary authority to share prisoner tax return information expired on December 31, 2011. The IRS indicated that with the enactment of the new legislation, the previous MOUs could not be used because they did not reflect the expanded requirements included in the American Taxpayer Relief Act of 2012. Therefore, new agreements had to be executed with the Federal Bureau of Prisons and the State Departments of Corrections once the IRS was given permanent authority to share prisoner return information in January 2013.

The IRS has created an MOU template that reflects the requirements of the American Taxpayer Relief Act of 2012. The IRS finalized the MOU template in July 2013 but then subsequently revised the MOU template in February 2014 to reflect changes to the Safeguarding guidelines. IRS management stated that the significant delays in finalizing the MOU template resulted from the number of reviews, approval signatures, and overall routing process. The IRS is taking steps to document and improve these processes to minimize future delays.

Participation in the sharing of prisoner tax return information is voluntary on the part of the Federal Bureau of Prisons and State Departments of Corrections. As such, the IRS indicated that letters were sent to the Federal Bureau of Prisons, the State Departments of Corrections,[12] and each State Governor as well as the Mayor of Washington, D.C. These letters explain the law, solicit participation, and indicate that the IRS will be reaching out to request a point of contact. These letters were not sent until February 2014, more than one year after permanent authority was granted. IRS management stated that leadership changes and the review process contributed to the delay in sending the letters.

As of July 11, 2014, the IRS has received points of contact for the Federal Bureau of Prisons, Washington, D.C., and 44 State Departments of Corrections. The IRS has not received a point of contact from six States, but plans to continue to reach out to these States to establish a point of contact. The ***********2******* is the only State that has signed an MOU. Three additional States are currently in the process of signing MOUs (********************2**********). Figure 3 illustrates the timeline of actions taken by the IRS subsequent to January 2013, when permanent authority to share information on false prisoner tax returns was granted.

Figure 3. Timeline of IRS Efforts to Share Prisoner Tax Return Data

Date	Event
January 2013	Legislation enacted that provides the IRS with permanent authority to share false prisoner tax return information with Federal and State prisons. IRS management establishes a cross-functional team to lead the developmentand execution of the MOU renewal strategy.
July 2013	The IRS finalizes the MOU template.

Figure 3. (Continued)

Date	Event
February 2014	The MOU template is revised to reflect new Safeguarding guidelines. The IRS sends solicitation letters to the Federal Bureau of Prisons, the State Departments of Corrections, the State Governors, and the Mayor of Washington, D.C.
March 2014	Field government liaisons begin contacting all State Departments of Corrections to establish a point of contact that the IRS can work with to begin the MOU process.
April 2014	The IRS secures the first signed MOU with the***************2********. The IRS also receives notification that the ********2*******declines to participate in the program due to the financial burden associated with carrying out the administrative actions and the limited Departments of Corrections benefits at this time.
July 2014	Three additional MOUs are in the approval process. The IRS is still working tosecure a point of contact for six States.

Source: IRS Return Integrity and Correspondence Services function.

Once an MOU is signed, meetings to support the State Departments of Corrections in completing the Safeguard Security Report can begin. These reports are required to be completed before any data will be shared. The reports detail the specific processes, procedures, and security controls in place to protect Federal tax information. As of July 2014, no Safeguard Security Reports have been completed.

Recommendation

Recommendation 1: The Commissioner, Wage and Investment Division, should ensure that points of contact for the remaining six State Departments of Corrections are obtained and ensure that MOUs are timely established with the Federal Bureau of Prisons and all State Departments of Corrections that have indicated an interest in receiving false prisoner tax return information.

Management's Response: The IRS agreed with this recommendation. As of August 1, 2014, the IRS has identified points of contact for all State Departments of Corrections. The IRS stated that it is committed to securing signed MOUs with the Federal Bureau of Prisons and the State Departments of

Corrections indicating interest in receiving information on false tax return information submitted by prisoners. According to the IRS, it is in discussions with 47 State Departments of Corrections, with 17 expressing an interest in signing an MOU. Because execution of an MOU is contingent on actions of other agencies, and is beyond the control of the IRS, the IRS did not commit to an additional corrective action in this regard.

Required Annual Prisoner Fraud Reports to Congress Are Not Timely and Do Not Address the Extent of Fraudulent Tax Return Filings by Prisoners

The IRS is not timely providing annual reports on the filing of fraudulent tax returns by Federal and State prisoners to Congress. The Inmate Tax Fraud Prevention Act of 2008 requires the Secretary of the Treasury to annually submit to Congress and make publicly available a report on the filing of false and fraudulent returns by individuals incarcerated in Federal and State prisons. Such a report shall include statistics on the number of false and fraudulent returns associated with each Federal and State prison. The first report completed by the IRS reported on tax returns filed using prisoner SSNs in Calendar Year 2009.

The IRS issued the Calendar Year 2009 report on the filing of false or fraudulent prisoner tax returns in September 2010. If the IRS had followed this general time frame for subsequent reports, it would have issued the Calendar Year 2010 report in September 2011, the Calendar Year 2011 report in September 2012, *etc.* However, the IRS did not issue the Calendar Year 2010 annual report until July 2012. The Calendar Year 2011 report was not issued until December 2013. As of June 30, 2014, the IRS has yet to issue the Calendar Year 2012 or Calendar Year 2013 required annual prisoner fraud reports. Figure 4 shows the time between the end of the calendar year and issuance of the annual prisoner tax fraud reports for Calendar Years 2009 through 2013.

In response to our concerns with the delays in issuing the annual prisoner fraud report, the IRS indicated that some delays were a result of the approval process and others were directly related to the data analysis process. The IRS also indicated that preparing the report to Congress is labor intensive and it has limited resources. IRS management stated that they are taking necessary steps to document the process in order to minimize these delays in the future.

Figure 4. Issuance of the Annual Prisoner Fraud Reports to Congress

Calendar Year Report	Date Issued to Congress	Months Elapsed Since theEnd of the Calendar Year
Calendar Year 2009	September 3, 2010	8
Calendar Year 2010	July 3, 2012	18
Calendar Year 2011	December 23, 2013	24
Calendar Year 2012	Not Issued as of June 2014	18
Calendar Year 2013	Not Issued as of June 2014	6

Source: TIGTA analysis of the IRS's Annual Reports to Congress.

To prepare the annual report, the IRS uses data contained in the EFDS. Most tax returns are screened and verified through the EFDS at the time the tax return is filed, which is generally between January and April each year. The IRS also tracks the number of potentially fraudulent prisoner tax returns it screens and/or verifies as well as those it confirms as fraudulent throughout the year. This information is reported weekly in internal IRS fraud reports, and we include it in our annual assessment of the individual tax return filing season.

Furthermore, the IRS has most of the information it needs to prepare the annual prisoner fraud report soon after the end of the calendar year. For example, IRS management indicated that each February (after the end of the previous calendar year) they obtain information from the EFDS that identifies tax returns filed using a prisoner SSN. The data are then manipulated in order to be able to report prisoner information by State and institution.

The Annual Prisoner Fraud Report Does Not Address the Extent of Tax Fraud Committed by Prisoners Using ****************2*** ****************

The law requires the IRS to provide an annual report on the filing of false or fraudulent tax returns by Federal and State prisoners. *****************2************************************2*** ***************. The report does not address the extent to which prisoners may be filing fraudulent tax returns***********2***************. For example, in the following tax fraud schemes, the prisoner is filing fraudulent tax returns ***********************2*******************and this type of fraud is not included in the annual report. The report will only include those tax returns filed*********2********.

On August 23, 2012, in Harrisburg, Pa., Theodore Scott, an inmate at Camp Hill Correctional Institution, was sentenced to 33 months in prison, three years of supervised release and ordered to pay $5,110 in restitution to the IRS for his role in a false claims tax scheme. Scott pleaded guilty to one count of conspiracy to defraud the United States by obtaining or aiding to obtain the payment of a false, fictitious or fraudulent claim. According to the indictment, Scott *obtained the social security numbers of other persons and used them to file false and fraudulent tax returns requesting refunds from the IRS.* Scott also filed false and fraudulent tax returns in his own name. These false tax returns declared fictitious income amounts and claimed fraudulent tax refunds. As part of the scheme, the refund checks were directed to the addresses of co-conspirators who would deposit them [into] bank accounts that Scott controlled.

On March 18, 2014, in Birmingham, Ala., Shermaine German was sentenced to 66 months in prison, three years of supervised release and ordered to pay $788,280 in restitution to the government. German pleaded guilty in December 2013 to a tax conspiracy. German, now paroled from state prison, was an inmate at Donaldson Correctional Facility in Bessemer when he orchestrated the tax scheme. According to court documents, from January 2008 to May 2013, while an inmate at Donaldson, German *obtained the names, birth dates and Social Security numbers of other people*, often fellow inmates. He used their information to create false income tax returns that contained fabricated amounts of tax withholdings. German also created false power of attorney forms, which he mailed out of the prison along with the false income tax returns. Various other members of the conspiracy notarized the power of attorney forms and used them to cash or deposit income tax refund checks received as part of the scheme.

To help determine the possible extent of the filing of false or fraudulent tax returns by Federal and State prisoners that is not included in the IRS's annual reports to Congress, we performed data analysis using the direct deposit number included on tax returns filed using a prisoner SSN. Our analysis of direct deposit information from the tax returns identified as fraudulent and filed using a prisoner SSN identified other individuals who used the same direct deposit number to receive a refund. For example, our analysis of the 579,592 tax returns that the IRS identified as being filed using a prisoner SSN found that 157,041 were determined to be fraudulent by the IRS. Of the 157,041 fraudulent prisoner tax returns, 157,025 claimed refunds. The IRS was not able to prevent the issuance of a refund for 16,449 fraudulent returns that used a direct deposit account. There were 16,342 unique direct deposit accounts used on these 16,449 tax returns.

Using the 16,342 direct deposit account numbers, we identified that 1,777 of the direct deposit account numbers were also used on another 47,321 tax returns. These 47,321 tax returns were filed*********2***** ********************. The tax refunds claimed on these tax returns totaled more than $102 million. For example, as Figure 5 shows, Bank Account A was used on a tax return filed with a prisoner SSN to receive a refund. The same bank account was also used on 7,645 additional tax returns. This type of analysis could assist the IRS in identifying characteristics of tax returns that may involve a prisoner refund scheme as well as the possible extent of the filing of false or fraudulent tax returns by Federal and State prisoners. Figure 5 shows the number of tax returns and amounts deposited into the top 10 direct deposit account numbers used in these situations.

**Figure 5. Top 10 Direct Deposit Account Numbers
Used on Both Prisoner and Nonprisoner Tax Returns**

Bank Account	Tax Returns Using the Same Direct Deposit Account As a Tax Return Filed by a Prisoner	Refunds Claimed
Bank Account A	7,645	$30,481,992
Bank Account B	1,855	$753,800
Bank Account C	1,840	$6,875,604
Bank Account D	1,740	$618,935
Bank Account E	1,174	$345,053
Bank Account F	1,124	$1,570,009
Bank Account G	1,065	$1,949,558
Bank Account H	871	$3,882,072
Bank Account I	797	$1,936,025
Bank Account J	734	$1,800,597

Source: TIGTA analysis of Processing Year[13] 2013 files.

Recommendations

The Commissioner, Wage and Investment Division, should:

Recommendation 2: Ensure that the required annual report on the filing of false or fraudulent tax returns by Federal and State prisoners is issued to

Congress timely. Given the availability of the data needed to compile the report, the report should be issued within nine months of the end of the applicable calendar year.

Management's Response: The IRS agreed with this recommendation. The IRS stated that it recognizes the need for timely submission of the annual prisoner fraud report to Congress and strives to compile complete and accurate data for its preparation. The IRS indicated that the source data for the report are obtained from the Scheme Tracking and Retrieval System, which contains the results of actions the IRS took in reviewing returns and determining probable fraud. Because return reviews must be completed before results are entered into the Scheme Tracking and Retrieval System, needed processing year-end data are not available until the following February or later.

According to the IRS, compiling and analyzing the data is a labor intensive process that must be performed before the report is drafted. In addition, the report is subjected to a a rigorous internal review as well as review by the Department of the Treasury, the Office of Management and Budget, and other affected agencies before submission to Congress. For the Calendar Year 2014 Prisoner Fraud Report, for which the data will become available in February 2015, the IRS will benchmark the report preparation and review process with the goal of a September 30, 2015, report date. The IRS will review and evaluate its performance after the report is released to establish a reasonable and realistic reporting time frame and expected delivery date for future reports.

Recommendation 3: Develop processes to identify tax returns filed that have the same characteristics as confirmed fraudulent prisoner tax returns, including those fraudulent tax returns identified as part of the IRS's other fraud detection programs, and determine whether these tax returns should be included in the annual report to Congress.

Management's Response: The IRS did not agree with this recommendation. The IRS stated that the methodology used in the annual report to Congress is consistent with the methodology used in reports of previous years. It reports all known false and fraudulent returns filed by prisoners as required by the statute. The IRS stated that the characteristics upon which our recommendation relies are not sufficiently reliable to conclude that all the returns identified are filed by inmates. According to the IRS, inmates are frequently also victims of identity theft, which can lead to an overstatement of fraudulent returns filed by prisoners. To ensure accuracy in reporting, the IRS accounts for returns when there is more than a circumstantial relationship to the identified prisoner.

Office of Audit Comment: The IRS's annual report only includes false and fraudulent tax returns filed using the SSN of a prisoner. The report does not include, as required, information related to the filing of false and fraudulent tax returns by prisoners. The characteristics we provided in our report were used to show information that could be used by the IRS to better determine the possible extent of the filing of false or fraudulent tax returns by Federal and State prisoners that is not included in the IRS's annual reports to Congress.

Processes Do Not Ensure That All Tax Returns Filed Using a Prisoner Social Security Number Are Assigned a Prisoner Indicator

Our analysis of tax returns filed during Calendar Year 2013 identified 43,030 tax returns that were filed using a prisoner SSN that were not assigned a prisoner indicator. Tax returns not assigned prisoner indicators include:

- 16,950 (39 percent) paper tax returns that did not meet the IRS's criteria for inclusion in the EFDS. Unlike all electronically filed tax returns being processed through the EFDS, the IRS has established certain criteria that will result in some paper tax returns not being processed through the EFDS.

- 26,080 (61 percent) tax returns that did meet the criteria for processing through the EFDS but were not assigned a prisoner indicator. We provided these tax returns to IRS management for review. On June 26, 2014, management agreed that an SSN that was on the Prisoner File was used to file the tax return. The IRS subsequently indicated that it did not agree that a prisoner indicator should have been assigned for the majority of these tax returns because the return reported a balance due or zero balance. Notwithstanding the IRS's response, we identified other balance due tax returns that were assigned a prisoner indicator. Analysis of the Calendar Year 2013 EFDS data identified 2,518 tax returns filed using a prisoner SSN with a balance due and the IRS assigned a prisoner indicator to the tax return.

In addition, we identified another 3,139 tax returns filed using the SSN of a prisoner for which the IRS did not assign a prisoner indicator because the name on the tax return was not the same name associated with the SSN on the Prisoner File. However, we were able to match the name on the tax return with the name on the Prisoner File and asked the IRS why it could not match the names on the two files. The IRS's review of these tax returns identified that the majority resulted from a two-character field (included on "preprinted" address labels provided to the taxpayer by the IRS) being loaded into the EFDS instead of the actual name control. A name control is the first four letters in an individual's last name, *e.g.*, the name control for Smith would be SMIT, but the two-character field NJ was loaded into the EFDS. The IRS is working to determine the cause of these programming issues.

A prior TIGTA Review Found That Not All Tax Returns Filed Using the SSN of a Prisoner Were Assigned an Indicator

In December 2010, we reported that 54,410 tax returns filed during Calendar Year 2009 using a prisoner SSN did not receive a prisoner indicator. In that report, we recommended that the IRS ensure that all prisoner tax returns are processed through the EFDS and receive a prisoner indicator. In response to our recommendation, IRS management stated that the IRS has reviewed the process for identifying prisoner tax returns early in Calendar Year 2010, and changes were made that would improve the IRS's ability to identify those individuals who are incarcerated and assign a prisoner indicator to their account. When we questioned the IRS about the specific actions taken to improve the assignment of the prisoner indicator, it informed us that the process used to assign a prisoner indicator had not changed. As a result, the IRS still does not identify all tax returns filed using a prisoner SSN.

We are concerned that management has not taken action to address this issue which we have previously raised to their attention. The assignment of the indicator is an automated process within the EFDS whereby the primary and secondary name and the SSN on a filed tax return are compared to the names and SSNs listed in the Prisoner File. If a match is identified, a prisoner indicator is automatically set. All that is required is that the IRS processes all tax returns through the EFDS. As we have previously detailed, the IRS sets the specific criteria to be used to identify those tax returns with an indicator to be sent to screening and/or verification. For example, the IRS can exclude tax returns with a prisoner indicator that have a balance due from being sent to screening and/or verification.

When tax returns filed using a prisoner SSN are not assigned the required indicator, the tax return will not be subjected to the IRS's specialized prisoner fraud checks. All tax returns filed using a prisoner SSN should receive an indicator regardless of whether they appear fraudulent. The indicator should alert IRS employees who may be addressing other issues related to the tax return that the return was filed using a prisoner SSN.

Recommendations

The Commissioner, Wage and Investment Division, should:

Recommendation 4: Ensure that all tax returns that are filed using a prisoner SSN are assigned a prisoner indicator.

Management's Response: The IRS agreed with this recommendation to the extent that it agrees that all accounts for which a tax return is filed using a prisoner SSN should be identified. The IRS stated that the Master File displays that information for all prisoner accounts to alert IRS employees addressing other issues related to the tax return or to that account. The IRS disagreed that an indicator should be assigned to returns for EFDS screening when a refund is not being claimed.

Office of Audit Comment: The IRS incorrectly noted that the Master File could be used by IRS employees to identify tax returns filed using a prisoner SSN. Our research of the specific returns we identified found that not all of them were identified on the Master File. As we previously reported, we believe the IRS should assign a prisoner indicator to all prisoner tax returns. The assignment of a prisoner indicator is an automated process requiring the IRS to expend no additional resources to ensure that tax returns with a prisoner SSN are consistently assigned.

Recommendation 5: Identify and address the cause associated with the 26,080 tax returns filed using the SSN of a prisoner that were not identified with the prisoner indicator.

Management's Response: The IRS agreed with this recommendation. The IRS will review the refund returns included in the 26,080 exception cases to ascertain why they did not receive a prisoner indicator by the EFDS. The IRS indicated that the remainder were no-balance or balance due returns and will not be reviewed as they would not have been considered potential fraudulent refund returns.

Recommendation 6: Correct computer programming errors that resulted in not assigning a prisoner indicator to 3,139 tax returns because the name in the EFDS did not match the name associated with the SSN on the Prisoner File.

Management's Response: The IRS did not agree with this recommendation. The IRS stated that the condition that caused the 3,139 returns not to receive prisoner indicators by the EFDS is a systemic limitation caused by unperfected entity data included in the return record that is delivered to the EFDS. According to the IRS, the condition affected approximately three percent of transcribed paper returns. Other processing systems validate and perfect the data before the return information posts to the Master File, and the returns are still processed through the EFDS to screen them and assign a data mining score to assess fraud potential.

Office of Audit Comment: We agree that these tax returns were evaluated using other EFDS filters. However, without the proper assignment of a prisoner indicator, these tax returns are not sent through those filters specific to a prisoner-filed tax return.

APPENDIX I. DETAILED OBJECTIVE, SCOPE, AND METHODOLOGY

Our overall objective was to evaluate the effectiveness of the IRS's corrective actions to identify and reduce prisoner fraud. We conducted follow-up testing to evaluate the effectiveness of the IRS's actions to address recommendations made in a previous TIGTA report.[1] In addition, we evaluated the IRS's compliance with the continuing provisions of the Inmate Tax Fraud Prevention Act of 2008[2] and the American Taxpayer Relief Act of 2012.[3] To accomplish our objective, we:

I. Assessed the adequacy of the IRS's implementation of corrective actions in response to our prior audit.[4]

    A. Determined the improvements the IRS has made to the process to identify individuals who are incarcerated and assign prisoner indicators to the tax returns filed using an SSN that is included on the Prisoner File.

    B. Determined if these improvements corrected the previously reported conditions.

1) Performed data analysis using TIGTA's Data Center Warehouse5 Individual Return Transaction File6 and the Prisoner File to identify tax returns filed using an SSN on the Prisoner File in Processing Year7 2013.

2) Requested a data extract of the EFDS8 for all tax returns filed that have the prisoner indicator for Processing Year 2013.

3) Established the reliability of the computer-processed data from Steps I.B.1. and 2. In order to accomplish this, we compared the information from the various files and reviewed information from the IRS's Integrated Data Retrieval System9 and the Prisoner File. We determined that the data are sufficiently reliable for the purposes of this report.

4) Compared the files in Steps I.B.1. and 2. to determine if there are any returns in the EFDS data extract that were not identified in our data analysis. We determined why they were not in our data.

5) Compared the files in Steps I.B.1. and 2. to determine if all prisoner tax returns we identified are included in the EFDS data extract and have the prisoner indicator. For any returns we identified as prisoner returns that are not included in the EFDS data extract, we determined if they met the criteria to be processed through the EFDS.

II. Determined the status and effectiveness of the sharing of false or fraudulent tax returns filed by prisoners with the Federal and State prisons.

   A. Obtained copies of the completed MOUs and determined if MOUs have been set up with all State Departments of Corrections and the Federal Bureau of Prisons.

   B. Determined what, if any, data have been shared with prisons.

III. Assessed the IRS's compliance with the Inmate Tax Fraud Prevention Act of 2008 requirement to provide an annual report on prisoner fraud to Congress.

   A. Determined if the IRS timely provided a report for Calendar Years 2009 through 2013 to the Department of the Treasury for review and subsequently to Congress.

   B. Performed data analysis using the EFDS data extract provided by the IRS and TIGTA's Data Center Warehouse Refund File[10] to identify tax returns requesting direct deposits into the same accounts as fraudulent returns filed with prisoner SSNs in Processing Year 2013. We established the reliability of the Refund

File by comparing the information in the file to the IRS's Integrated Data Retrieval System. We determined that the data are sufficiently reliable for the purposes of this report.

Internal Controls Methodology

Internal controls relate to management's plans, methods, and procedures used to meet their mission, goals, and objectives. Internal controls include the processes and procedures for planning, organizing, directing, and controlling program operations. They include the systems for measuring, reporting, and monitoring program performance. We determined that the following internal controls were relevant to our audit objective: ensuring that the provisions of the Inmate Tax Fraud Prevention Act of 2008 and the American Taxpayer Relief Act of 2012 were implemented, identifying and evaluating the validity of the assignment of the prisoner indicator, and verifying that certain returns with prisoner SSNs are subject to compliance treatments. We evaluated these controls by obtaining information from IRS management about the status of data sharing with the Federal Bureau of Prisons and with the States and about the status of the annual prisoner fraud report to Congress. We analyzed data received from the IRS's EFDS as well as the Individual Return Transaction File and the Prisoner File from TIGTA's Data Center Warehouse to determine whether the prisoner indicators were being assigned correctly and whether certain returns were being reviewed.

APPENDIX II. MAJOR CONTRIBUTORS TO THIS REPORT

Russell P. Martin, Acting Assistant Inspector General for Audit (Returns Processing and Account Services)
Deann L. Baiza, Director
Sharla J. Robinson, Audit Manager
Karen C. Fulte, Lead Auditor
Linda L. Bryant, Senior Auditor
Steven D. Stephens, Senior Auditor

APPENDIX III. REPORT DISTRIBUTION LIST

Commissioner C
Office of the Commissioner – Attn: Chief of Staff C
Deputy Commissioner for Services and Enforcement SE
Chief, Criminal Investigation SE:CI
Deputy Chief, Criminal Investigation SE:CI
Deputy Commissioner, Wage and Investment Division SE:W
Director, Return Integrity and Correspondence Services SE:W:RICS
Chief Counsel CC
National Taxpayer Advocate TA
Director, Office of Legislative Affairs CL:LA
Director, Office of Program Evaluation and Risk Analysis RAS:O
Office of Internal Control OS:CFO:CPIC:IC
Audit Liaison: Director, Return Integrity and Correspondence Services
    SE:W:RICS

APPENDIX IV. EXAMPLE LETTER SENT TO STATE DEPARTMENTS OF CORRECTIONS

DEPARTMENT OF THE TREASURY
INTERNAL REVENUE SERVICE
ATLANTA, GA 30308

COMMISSIONER
WAGE AND INVESTMENT DIVISION

FEB 0 3 2014

Secretary
Department of Corrections

Dear Secretary

We are committed to doing everything possible to stop inmate tax fraud, and we need your assistance again. One of the most important actions we take to fight this type of tax fraud is work with State corrections officials

2

The information prison officials provide annually allows us to identify false or fraudulent inmate returns. In 2011, we identified over 186,000 Federal tax returns filed by inmates that claimed over $3.7 billion in false or fraudulent refunds. Inmates in your State prisons filed over ████ fraudulent Federal tax returns that claimed over ████████ in refunds. Today, I'm asking you to take another step to reduce these claims and stop fraudulent tax refunds from entering our prison systems.

The previous temporary authority that allowed us to disclose information to you under a Memorandum of Understanding expired on December 31, 2011. On January 2, 2013, as part of the American Taxpayer Relief Act of 2012, the Congress made permanent our authority to disclose prisoner information to State and Federal prison officials when we determine a prisoner may have filed or helped file a false or fraudulent tax return. The Congress also added the following disclosure authorities for the purpose of taking administrative actions to prevent prisoners from filing false or fraudulent returns:

- The IRS can disclose information directly to employees and officers of a prison and to contractors responsible for operating a prison.
- The IRS can disclose copies of Federal tax returns to prison officials.
- A prison official can re-disclose an inmate's tax returns and return information to the prison's legal representative and the inmate's legal representative for administrative and judicial proceedings arising from the prison's administrative action.

The law's enhancements and permanent status addresses a number of challenges prison officials told us they faced with implementing the previous authorization. The added disclosure authorities are a dramatic improvement to the Disclosure Program.

For your convenience, we enclosed the history of the law authorizing disclosure of inmate tax fraud.

While I am counting on your support, I recognize the difficult fiscal situations facing the State governments. You have my commitment that we will work with you and your staff to identify practical, cost-effective ways to implement this program. In the coming days, the IRS governmental liaison for your state will contact your office to provide more information about this program. In addition, he or she will request a point of contact to set up a subsequent call to discuss this program with you or members of your staff.

Thank you for your continued partnership and support. If you have any questions, please contact me or a member of your staff may contact ████████████ Chief, Return Integrity and Correspondence Services Project and Technology Management and Agency Coordinator, at ████████████.

Thank you for your cooperation.

Sincerely,

Peggy Bogadi

Enclosure

History of the Law Authorizing Disclosure of Inmate Tax Fraud

In an effort to curb inmate tax refund fraud, Congress enacted the Inmate Tax Fraud Prevention Act of 2008 (Public Law 110-428) to authorize the IRS to disclose to the Federal Bureau of Prisons all tax return information for federal inmates who the IRS determines may have filed or helped someone file a fraudulent return. The Federal Bureau of Prisons could only use the information for inmate disciplinary proceedings to address possible violations of prison rules and regulations. This authority was codified in the Internal Revenue Code at 26 U.S.C. § 6103(k)(10).

The Congress didn't authorize similar disclosures to State prison agencies until the Homebuyer Assistance and Improvement Act of 2010 (Public Law 111-198). This Act amended 26 U.S.C. § 6103(k)(10) to authorize the IRS to disclose return information about fraudulent inmate returns to State agencies charged with the responsibility for administration of prisons. Just as with their Federal counterpart, the State agencies could only use the information in inmate disciplinary proceedings.

To initiate the Disclosure Program, the IRS, the Federal Bureau of Prisons, and various State departments of correction signed agreements in 2010 and 2011 on the disclosure process.

On December 31, 2011, our authorization to disclose return information expired.

On January 2, 2013, as part of the American Taxpayer Relief Act of 2012 (Public Law 112-240), the Congress authorized an enhanced disclosure authority in 26 U.S.C. § 6103(k)(10) that gives the IRS permanent authority to disclose return information about fraudulent inmate returns to State prison agencies and the Federal Bureau of Prisons.

APPENDIX V. MANAGEMENT'S RESPONSE TO THE DRAFT REPORT

DEPARTMENT OF THE TREASURY
INTERNAL REVENUE SERVICE
ATLANTA, GA 30308

SEP 0 5 2014

MEMORANDUM FOR MICHAEL E. MCKENNEY
                          DEPUTY INSPECTOR GENERAL FOR AUDIT

FROM: Debra Holland   *Debra J. Holland*
                          Commissioner, Wage and Investment Division

2

SUBJECT: Draft Audit Report – Prisoner Tax Refund Fraud: Delays
                            Continue in Completing Agreements to Share Information With
                            Prisons and Reports to Congress Are Not Timely or Complete
                            (Audit # 201340016)

We appreciate the opportunity to review the subject draft report and provide comments.
The IRS has continued to build on processes to detect and stop potentially fraudulent
refund claims made by prisoners. We have worked with the Federal Bureau of Prisons
and State Departments of Correction to improve the quality and reliability of data used
in compiling the annual file of incarcerated individuals. The file is used by our major
processing systems to identify returns filed using prisoner Social Security Numbers
(SSN), to identify potential fraud and other compliance issues affected by an individual's
incarceration status. It is also used to alert IRS employees of that status when they are
addressing other account issues beyond the processing of tax returns. We are working
to establish Memoranda of Understanding (MOU) with the Federal Bureau of Prisons
and the State Departments of Correction to strengthen our detection and prevention
efforts by sharing fraudulent prisoner tax return information, as permitted by law. We
have held conferences with the Federal Bureau of Prisons and 19 State Departments of
Correction, and are scheduling meetings with the remainder. However, the execution of
the MOUs is dependent upon their agreements.

The IRS had temporary authority to disclose prisoner tax return information to prison
officials when fraud was suspected. Although that authority expired on December 31,
2011, and was not permanently reinstated until January 2013, the IRS continued to
engage the Federal Bureau of Prisons and State Departments of Correction through
other activities that allowed the IRS to receive information from the prisons on a
voluntary basis. We held discussions with federal officials, the District of Columbia, and
all states to explain the programs available to them that would reduce prisoner tax
fraud. These programs included limiting access to tax forms, education on anti-tax fraud
activities outside the scope of the MOUs, and the Blue Bag Program. Educational topics
included information on preventing the most common inmate refund fraud schemes
such as false or inflated wages or fictitious business income to receive false refunds
and/or refundable credits. We provided guest speakers at several American
Correctional Association conferences to address prevention of inmate tax fraud, and we
provided subject matter experts for the Federal Bureau of Prison's investigator training
on frivolous returns and inmate tax fraud. Posters advising prisoners of the ramifications
of conviction for tax related offensives were provided to federal and state prisons for
display. The Blue Bag program is a method for prisons to identify for review and/or
treatment tax returns, correspondence and other tax-related documents associated with
prisoners. With this program, states can send suspicious tax-related documents to the
IRS for appropriate follow up actions.

The IRS participated in discussions with federal and state officials, and noted their
concerns regarding administering a prisoner fraud prevention program. Based on these
conversations, proposed legislation was drafted to address those concerns and was
provided to Congress for consideration. The IRS proposals were included in the
American Taxpayer Relief Act of 2012 (ATRA) enacted in January 2013. The ATRA
provided permanent authority for the IRS to disclose tax returns and tax return
information directly to officers and employees of the federal or state prison agencies. It
also provided for disclosure to contractors operating prisons and re-disclosure by them
to legal representatives of the prisons and/or contractors to defend against inmate
appeals.

3

The Treasury Inspector General for Tax Administration (TIGTA) report does not accurately describe how the IRS uses prisoner information in identifying accounts and processing original and amended tax returns, or in responding to inquiries or other types of correspondence from taxpayers. The same source data file containing prisoner information is used by the Electronic Fraud Detection System (EFDS), Dependent Database, and Master File; however, each system has its own copy of the file and the data is used for different purposes. The prisoner data loaded into the EFDS is further refined to eliminate records where the name control associated with the SSN does not match the name control for that number in the Master File database. This is done to eliminate potentially erroneous records that could cause returns to be flagged as prisoner returns in error. Any return meeting the EFDS review criteria that does not get flagged for prisoner screening undergoes the normal data mining process for assessing fraud potential.

The report also cites our response to your previous recommendation, where IRS management stated the process for identifying prisoner tax returns had been reviewed early in Calendar Year 2010, and changes were made to improve the IRS's ability to identify those individuals who were incarcerated and assign a prisoner indicator to their account. It is correct that the prisoner assignment indicator process has not changed since the prior report. However, we also stated in that response that the changes were made in the screening selection process. New rules and filters that focus on the identification of full year prisoners result in more efficient use of resources. Further, the assignment of a prisoner indicator in EFDS affects only the treatment of that return within EFDS, and is not information that is queried or used by other employees in working with taxpayer accounts.

It is also important to note that there are numerous ways a prisoner could earn income while incarcerated. Prisoners, like all other taxpayers, are responsible for paying federal income taxes on all taxable income. Also, some prisoners continue to have investments and businesses operating while they are in prison. They are receiving income from these investments/businesses in the form of distributions, dividends, interest, and other income. Depending on the amount of these earnings, these prisoners may be required to file a tax return and may be entitled to a tax refund. For those fulfilling their filing obligations and not claiming refunds, it is not a productive use of our resources to designate those returns as potentially fraudulent refund schemes.

We acknowledge the TIGTA's point that all tax returns filed using a prisoner SSN should receive an indicator regardless of whether they appear fraudulent. Although the EFDS applies more restrictive criteria in assigning prisoner indicators to the returns it evaluates, the prisoner status indicator attaches to all prisoner accounts in the Master File, regardless of the EFDS treatment of returns filed by those taxpayers. The prisoner designation is available to IRS employees addressing other account issues of these individuals.

Attached is our response to your recommendations. If you have any questions, please contact me, or a member of your staff may contact Jodi L. Patterson, Return Integrity and Correspondence Services, Wage and Investment Division, at (404) 338-8961.

Attachment

Recommendation

RECOMMENDATION 1
The Commissioner, Wage and Investment Division, should ensure that points of contact for the remaining six State Departments of Corrections are obtained and ensure that MOUs are timely established with the Federal Bureau of Prisons and all State Departments of Corrections that have indicated an interest in receiving false prisoner tax return information.

CORRECTIVE ACTION
As of August 1, 2014, points of contact have been identified for all State Departments of Correction. The IRS is committed to securing signed Memoranda of Understanding (MOU) with the Federal Bureau of Prisons and the State Departments of Correction indicating interest in receiving information on false tax return information submitted by prisoners. We are in discussions with 47 State Departments of Correction, with 17 expressing an interest in signing an MOU. We will continue to work toward obtaining signed MOUs with the Federal Bureau of Prisons and all interested State Departments of Correction. Since execution of an MOU is contingent on actions of other agencies, and is beyond the control of the IRS, we do not commit to an additional corrective action in this regard.

IMPLEMENTATION DATE
Implemented

RESPONSIBLE OFFICIAL
Director, Return Integrity and Correspondence Services, Wage and Investment Division

CORRECTIVE ACTION MONITORING PLAN
N/A

Recommendations

The Commissioner, Wage and Investment Division, should:

RECOMMENDATION 2
Ensure that the required annual report on the filing of false or fraudulent tax returns by Federal and State prisoners is issued to Congress timely. Given the availability of the data needed to compile the report, the report should be issued within nine months of the end of the applicable calendar year.

CORRECTIVE ACTION
The IRS recognizes the need for timely submission of the Annual Prisoner Fraud Reports to Congress and strives to compile complete and accurate data for its preparation. The source data for the report is obtained from the Scheme Tracking and

2

Retrieval System (STARS), which contains the results of actions the IRS took in reviewing returns and determining probable fraud. Since return reviews must be completed before results are entered into STARS, needed processing year-end data is not available until the following February, or later. Compiling and analyzing the data is a labor intensive process that must be performed before the report is drafted. Recognizing the importance of the information being reported to Congress, a rigorous internal review process is performed. Additionally, the report is further reviewed by the Department of Treasury, the Office of Management and Budget, and other affected agencies before submission to Congress. For the Calendar Year 2014 Prisoner Fraud Report, for which the data will become available in February 2015, we will benchmark the report preparation and review process, with the goal of a September 30, 2015 report date. Performance will be reviewed and evaluated after the report is released to establish a reasonable and realistic reporting timeframe and expected delivery date for future reports.

IMPLEMENTATION DATE
February 15, 2016

RESPONSIBLE OFFICIAL
Director, Return Integrity and Correspondence Services, Wage and Investment Division

CORRECTIVE ACTION MONITORING PLAN
We will monitor this corrective action as part of our internal management control system.

RECOMMENDATION 3
Develop processes to identify tax returns filed that have the same characteristics as confirmed fraudulent prisoner tax returns, including those fraudulent tax returns identified as part of the IRS's other fraud detection programs, and determine whether these tax returns should be included in the annual report to Congress.

CORRECTIVE ACTION
The methodology used in the annual report to Congress is consistent with the methodology used in reports of previous years. As required by the statute, the IRS reports all known false and fraudulent returns filed by prisoners. The characteristics upon which the recommendation relies are not sufficiently reliable to conclude that all the returns identified are inmate-filed. Frequently, inmates are also victims of identity theft, which can lead to an overstatement of fraudulent returns filed by prisoners. To ensure accuracy in reporting, the IRS accounts for returns when there is more than a circumstantial relationship to the identified prisoner. We disagree with the recommendation.

IMPLEMENTATION DATE
N/A

3

RESPONSIBLE OFFICIAL
N/A

CORRECTIVE ACTION MONITORING PLAN
N/A

Recommendations

The Commissioner, Wage and Investment Division, should:

RECOMMENDATION 4
Ensure that all tax returns that are filed using a prisoner SSN are assigned a prisoner indicator.

CORRECTIVE ACTION
We agree with this recommendation to the extent that all accounts for which a tax return is filed using a prisoner Social Security Number should be identified. The Master File displays that information for all prisoner accounts, to alert IRS employees addressing other issues relating to the tax return or to that account. We disagree an indicator should be assigned to returns for Electronic Fraud Detection System (EFDS) screening when a refund is not being claimed.

IMPLEMENTATION DATE
N/A

RESPONSIBLE OFFICIAL
N/A

CORRECTIVE ACTION MONITORING PLAN
N/A

RECOMMENDATION 5
Identify and address the cause associated with the 26,080 tax returns filed using the SSN of a prisoner that were not identified with the prisoner indicator.

CORRECTIVE ACTION
We will review the refund returns included in the 26,080 exception cases to ascertain why they did not receive a prisoner indicator by the EFDS. The remainder were no-balance or balance due returns, which will not be reviewed as they would not have been considered potential fraudulent refund returns.

IMPLEMENTATION DATE
October 15, 2015

RESPONSIBLE OFFICIAL
Director, Return Integrity and Correspondence Services, Wage and Investment Division

CORRECTIVE ACTION MONITORING PLAN
We will monitor this corrective action as part of our internal management control system.

4

RECOMMENDATION 6:
Correct computer programming errors that resulted in not assigning a prisoner indicator to 3,139 tax returns because the name in the EFDS did not match the name associated with the SSN on the Prisoner File.

CORRECTIVE ACTION
The condition that caused the 3,139 returns not to receive prisoner indicators by the EFDS is a systemic limitation caused by unperfected entity data included in the return record that is delivered to the EFDS. The condition affected approximately three percent of transcribed paper returns; however, other processing systems validate and perfect the data before the return information posts to the Master File, and the returns are still processed through the EFDS to screen them and assign a data mining score to assess fraud potential. Therefore, we do not agree with this recommendation.

IMPLEMENTATION DATE
N/A

RESPONSIBLE OFFICIAL
N/A

CORRECTIVE ACTION MONITORING PLAN
N/A

End Notes

[1] Calendar Years 2010 and 2012 refund amounts do not add up due to rounding.

[2] The IRS indicated that this figure includes 468 returns filed by prisoners requesting refunds of more than $100,000 and totaling $2.9 billion. This is what caused the marked increase in refunds claimed in Calendar Year 2011.

[3] Pub. L. No. 110-428, 122 Stat. 4839.

[4] Pub. L. No. 111-198, 124 Stat. 1356.

[5] General term used to refer to the various State agencies that oversee State prisons.

[6] Pub. L. No. 112-41, § 502

[7] Pub. L. No. 112-240, 126 Stat. 2313.

[8] TIGTA, Ref. No. 2011-40-009, Significant Problems Still Exist With Internal Revenue Service Efforts to Identify Prisoner Tax Refund Fraud (Dec. 2010).

[9] TIGTA, Ref. No. 2013-40-011, Further Efforts Are Needed to Ensure the Internal Revenue Service Prisoner File Is Accurate and Complete (Dec. 2012).

[10] As noted on page 2 of the report, the American Taxpayer Relief Act of 2012, enacted January 2013, has given the IRS permanent authority to disclose this information to the prisons.

[11] The American Taxpayer Relief Act of 2012 expanded the scope of sharing to allow disclosure of false prisoner tax returns and tax return information to contractors of State and Federal prison facilities, during a judicial or administrative proceeding, and to the representatives of the prisoner involved in such proceedings.

[12] See Appendix IV for an example of the letter sent to the State Departments of Corrections.

[13] The calendar year in which the tax return or document is processed by the IRS.

End Notes for Appendix I

[1] TIGTA, Ref. No. 2011-40-009, Significant Problems Still Exist With Internal Revenue Service Efforts to Identify Prisoner Tax Refund Fraud (Dec. 2010).

[2] Pub. L. No. 110-428, 122 Stat. 4839.

[3] Pub. L. No. 112-240, 126 Stat. 2313.

[4] We did not perform audit work to assess the adequacy of the IRS corrective action for TIGTA, Ref. No. 2013-40-011, Further Efforts Are Needed to Ensure the Internal Revenue Service Prisoner File Is Accurate and Complete (Dec. 2012) because the implementation date for these actions was in April 2014.

[5] The Data Center Warehouse provides data and data access services through the TIGTA intranet.

[6] The Individual Return Transaction File contains data transcribed from initial input of the original individual tax returns during return processing.

[7] The calendar year in which the tax return or document is processed by the IRS.

[8] The EFDS consists of a series of filters the IRS has designed to evaluate tax returns for potential fraud. It is the primary system used by the IRS to identify tax returns filed using prisoner SSNs.

[9] The IRS computer system capable of retrieving or updating stored information. It works in conjunction with a taxpayer's account records.

[10] The Refund File captures all refunds which are sent by the IRS to the Bureau of the Fiscal Service for processing. The refunds are sent by the Bureau of the Fiscal Service to the taxpayers in the form of bank account direct deposits or mailed paper checks.

INDEX

A

abuse, 93, 96
access, 3, 10, 16, 17, 35, 75, 119
agencies, 11, 12, 40, 41, 51, 65, 99, 103, 118
Appropriations Act, 82
assessment, 3, 52, 54, 58, 65, 68, 69, 93, 100
audit, 6, 22, 31, 34, 35, 45, 71, 78, 82, 88, 95, 107, 109, 119
authentication, vii, viii, 39, 40, 41, 44, 46, 47, 51, 60, 61, 62, 63, 64, 65, 66, 67, 68, 70, 73, 75, 77, 83, 84
authority, 2, 3, 22, 27, 77, 90, 91, 93, 95, 96, 97, 118
automate, 73
awareness, 26

B

banking, 33, 37, 71
banks, 32, 70
benefits, 2, 4, 12, 17, 18, 19, 20, 21, 22, 26, 27, 28, 40, 41, 43, 58, 62, 65, 66, 67, 77, 98
budget cuts, 28, 82
budgetary resources, 19
business processes, 29
businesses, 22

C

cash, 101
category d, 54, 57
Census, 36
challenges, 2, 6, 13, 16, 18, 19, 20, 32, 40, 45, 46, 47, 59, 70
Chief of Staff, 110
citizens, 51, 80
clusters, 10, 49, 74
community, 25
compensation, 18, 74
complement, 11
complexity, 40, 46
compliance, 2, 7, 8, 9, 11, 16, 22, 34, 45, 49, 76, 82, 107, 108, 109
computer, 19, 20, 43, 45, 60, 75, 81, 84, 89, 107, 108, 119
computer systems, 45
Congress, v, 2, 3, 13, 16, 20, 22, 26, 27, 28, 35, 36, 41, 59, 65, 66, 77, 87, 88, 91, 92, 93, 95, 99, 100, 101, 103, 104, 108, 109
congressional requests, 94
conspiracy, 101
cost, vii, viii, 3, 15, 19, 22, 26, 39, 40, 41, 44, 53, 54, 55, 57, 59, 60, 61, 65, 66, 67, 68, 69, 70, 77, 81, 83, 84, 93
cost saving, 3, 22
cost-benefit analysis, 70

credentials, 63, 84
crimes, 46
criminal investigations, 14, 30, 60
criminals, 30, 43
critical infrastructure, 37
customer service, 76
cybersecurity, 37

D

data analysis, 99, 101, 108
data collection, 25
data mining, 107
database, 33
decision makers, 13, 59, 66, 67
Department of Justice, 45, 46
Department of the Treasury, 1, 3, 16, 42, 76, 93, 96, 103, 108
deposit accounts, 102
deposits, 108, 119
detection, 15, 16, 23, 24, 25, 27, 36, 49, 50, 52, 72, 76, 82, 89, 103
detection system, 23, 27
disclosure, 24, 36, 91, 96, 118
distribution, 63, 79
District of Columbia, 10, 21, 61
draft, 28, 29, 41, 64, 65, 67

E

earnings, 21
efficient resource allocation, 41, 65
employees, 18, 20, 21, 34, 35, 36, 47, 106
employers, vii, 2, 3, 4, 5, 7, 9, 16, 18, 19, 20, 21, 26, 28, 31, 34, 35, 36, 43, 48, 76
employment, 6, 21, 22, 31, 68, 81
enforcement, 34, 76
environment, 83
evidence, 6, 34, 45, 52, 53, 54, 55, 56, 69, 70, 71, 95
execution, 97, 99
Executive Order, 82
expertise, 32, 70

F

false positive, 10, 18, 19
family members, 47
federal government, 20, 12, 34, 68
filters, 6, 10, 13, 18, 29, 34, 35, 36, 47, 49, 52, 61, 62, 63, 65, 66, 74, 80, 83, 89, 92, 94, 107, 119
financial, vii, viii, 2, 4, 5, 6, 9, 10, 13, 15, 23, 24, 25, 31, 32, 33, 37, 40, 44, 48, 70, 71, 75, 76, 98
financial institutions, vii, viii, 2, 5, 6, 9, 11, 13, 15, 23, 25, 31, 32, 37, 40, 44, 48, 70, 75, 76
fraudulent tax return, vii, viii, 2, 4, 6, 39, 43, 45, 66, 87, 88, 89, 90, 91, 99, 100, 101, 102, 103, 104, 108
funding, 16
funds, 15, 60

G

GAO, vii, viii, 1, 2, 3, 6, 7, 8, 9, 12, 17, 33, 34, 35, 36, 37, 39, 40, 41, 42, 44, 46, 48, 50, 51, 52, 53, 54, 55, 56, 57, 58, 61, 67, 68, 69, 71, 72, 74, 75, 76, 77, 78, 79, 80, 81, 82, 83, 84
Georgia, 10, 61, 95
guidance, 41, 44, 60, 65, 67, 70, 84
guidelines, 44, 52, 68, 81, 82, 84, 97, 98
guilty, 101

H

history, 13
House, 4, 33, 43, 71
House of Representatives, 4, 43
human, 19

I

identification, 9, 43, 44, 60, 61, 62, 66, 68, 70, 72, 75, 81, 84

identity, vii, 1, 2, 4, 5, 6, 7, 8, 9, 10, 11, 15,
    21, 26, 29, 31, 36, 39, 42, 43, 44, 45, 46,
    47, 49, 51, 58, 60, 61, 62, 63, 64, 68, 70,
    72, 74, 75, 76, 77, 80, 81, 82, 83, 84, 94,
    103
Identity theft tax refund fraud, vii, 2
Identity Theft Taxonomy, vii, 1, 2, 5, 12,
    29, 31, 42, 44, 49, 50, 54, 56, 68, 77
improvements, 15, 28, 31, 53, 55, 107
income, 7, 11, 18, 23, 42, 49, 51, 53, 54, 61,
    62, 72, 76, 92, 101
income tax, 23, 101
individual taxpayers, 24
individuals, 30, 45, 62, 63, 80, 91, 92, 94,
    95, 99, 101, 105, 107
industry, 37, 60, 68
information sharing, 28, 96
information technology, 19, 35, 58, 60
inmates, 101, 103
institutions, 6, 24, 25, 32, 37, 70
integrity, 4
internal controls, 12, 20, 22, 24, 109
Internal Revenue Service, 1, 2, 4, 31, 35, 37,
    40, 42, 43, 68, 72, 77, 83, 87, 90, 118,
    119
investment(s), 26, 28, 37, 43, 62
issues, 3, 7, 8, 16, 19, 32, 34, 36, 45, 46, 70,
    72, 76, 82, 105, 106

L

laptop, 43, 60, 81, 84
lead, 10, 25, 27, 28, 37, 40, 66, 77, 97, 103
leadership, 97
learning, 15
legislation, 93, 95, 96
legislative proposals, 32
life cycle, 50, 53
light, 5, 46
low risk, 83

M

magnitude, 19, 79

majority, 104, 105
management, 11, 20, 22, 24, 37, 41, 53, 55,
    57, 64, 69, 93, 96, 97, 99, 100, 104, 105,
    109
mapping, 65
matrix, 5, 29, 50
methodology, viii, 5, 6, 13, 14, 31, 32, 35,
    40, 44, 45, 52, 53, 54, 55, 56, 68, 69, 70,
    77, 95, 103
mission(s), 11, 109
misuse, 84
models, 74
modernization, 33, 37, 71

N

National Security Council, 51
National Strategy, 42, 83

O

Obama, 82
objectivity, 52
Office of Management and Budget, 41, 42,
    44, 51, 68, 103
OMB, 42, 44, 51, 52, 65, 67, 68, 70, 81, 82,
    83, 84
operations, 22, 109
opportunities, 5, 17, 32, 37
opportunity costs, 36
oversight, 93

P

parallel, 35
password, 63, 84
payroll, vii, 2, 6, 18, 20, 21, 23, 36
penalties, 18
perpetrators, 5
playing, 66
policy, 20, 25, 33, 71
policymakers, 5, 13, 41, 57
population, 63, 81
potential benefits, 11, 66

preparation, 33, 71, 103
President, 35
prevention, 11, 20, 23, 27, 66, 76
prisoner fraud, viii, 88, 92, 93, 99, 100, 103,
    106, 107, 108, 109
prisoners, 34, 82, 88, 89, 90, 91, 92, 93, 94,
    95, 96, 99, 100, 101, 102, 103, 104, 108,
    118
prisons, 91, 93, 94, 95, 97, 99, 108, 118
professionals, 11, 83
programming, 89, 105, 107
project, 35
protection, 37, 64
Puerto Rico, 21

R

random numbers, 63
recommendations, 2, 28, 40, 43, 64, 67, 77,
    88, 93, 107
relative size, 59
reliability, 32, 34, 52, 53, 55, 67, 82, 93, 94,
    108
requirements, 24, 36, 96, 97
resolution, 75, 82
resources, 2, 3, 12, 21, 24, 25, 26, 28, 40,
    41, 47, 52, 57, 59, 63, 66, 67, 99, 106
response, 5, 24, 47, 56, 64, 83, 95, 99, 104,
    105, 107
restitution, 101
restrictions, 27, 37
revenue, 18, 19, 44, 46, 67, 68
risk(s), 11, 18, 20, 24, 26, 37, 40, 41, 47, 49,
    54, 58, 64, 65, 66, 67, 69, 75, 83
risk factors, 11
risk management, 11, 24
rules, 54, 57, 69

S

SAS, 33, 71
savings, 3, 20
scope, 6, 26, 44, 45, 67, 95, 118
Secretary of the Treasury, 27, 77, 90, 91, 99

security, 44, 46, 51, 63, 65, 96, 98
Senate, 4, 35, 42
sensitivity, 54, 55, 58, 59, 68, 69, 78, 82, 84
services, 33, 37, 64, 71, 119
showing, 57, 58
silver, 26, 43
small businesses, 21
Social Security, viii, 1, 3, 6, 7, 16, 32, 34,
    42, 46, 72, 77, 81, 82, 87, 88, 90, 101,
    104
Social Security Administration, 1, 3, 6, 16,
    32, 34, 77, 82
software, vii, viii, 2, 6, 19, 20, 23, 24, 25,
    40, 44, 60, 61, 62, 70, 75, 83
specific tax, 37
spreadsheets, 25
SSA, vii, 1, 2, 3, 6, 7, 16, 18, 19, 20, 21, 22,
    27, 28, 32, 34, 35, 36
staffing, 47
stakeholders, 6, 11, 13, 15, 19, 20, 24, 26,
    28, 32, 44, 49, 60, 65, 70
state(s), 21, 36, 41, 46, 54, 64, 101
statistics, 99
strategic planning, 11

T

tactics, 15
target, 16, 43, 45, 63
tax administration, vii, viii, 2, 4, 22, 25, 28,
    46, 62, 64, 87, 90
tax return data, 34, 48, 76, 83
tax system, 4, 43, 46, 93, 96
taxes, 18, 63, 73
taxpayer authentication, vii, viii, 39, 40, 44,
    60, 62, 66, 67, 68, 70
taxpayers, vii, viii, 2, 3, 4, 7, 10, 11, 16, 18,
    21, 22, 23, 26, 27, 28, 30, 34, 36, 40, 41,
    43, 44, 45, 46, 47, 49, 57, 60, 61, 62, 63,
    64, 65, 66, 68, 72, 73, 74, 77, 79, 83, 119
technical comments, 28, 29, 40, 67
techniques, 44, 65
technologies, 47
technology, 25, 37, 65
telephone, 64

testing, 5, 32, 34, 44, 52, 53, 55, 65, 69, 82, 107

theft, vii, 1, 2, 4, 5, 10, 11, 29, 31, 36, 39, 42, 43, 46, 51, 68, 72, 74, 75, 77, 80, 82, 103

third-party information, vii, 2, 5, 9, 31, 43, 46, 62

time frame, 51, 99, 103

tracks, 82, 100

transactions, 63, 65, 73

transcription, 22

transmission, 61

Treasury, v, 1, 2, 3, 16, 19, 20, 22, 26, 32, 35, 36, 42, 77, 82, 87, 90, 92

U

U.S. Treasury, 28

unions, 32, 70

United States, v, 1, 4, 39, 42, 91, 101

universe, 30

updating, 12, 19, 29, 64, 119

V

validation, 94

victims, 5, 9, 47, 61, 63, 66, 72, 103

vision, 82

vulnerability, 45

W

W-2s, vii, 2, 3, 7, 9, 14, 15, 16, 17, 18, 19, 20, 21, 22, 27, 28, 32, 33, 34, 35, 36, 77

wages, 17, 74, 94

Washington, 34, 35, 37, 81, 82, 83, 84, 85, 97, 98

web, 22, 35

White House, 83

workload, 18, 82

wrongdoing, 93